GEORGE RAYNOR

GEORGE RAYNOR

THE GREATEST COACH ENGLAND NEVER HAD

ASHLEY HYNE

First published 2014

The History Press
The Mill, Brimscombe Port
Stroud, Gloucestershire, GL5 2QG
www.thehistorypress.co.uk

British Library Cataloguing in Publication Data.
A catalogue record for this book is available from the British Library.

ISBN 978 0 7509 5967 4

Typesetting and origination by The History Press
Printed in Great Britain

CONTENTS

	About the Author	6
	Acknowledgements	7
	Foreword by Gordon Pulley	9
	Introduction	19
1	The Early Years	22
2	A Playing Career Unfulfilled?	30
3	The War Years	47
4	Opportunities in Sweden	59
5	Olympic Gold	67
6	Olympic Glory	77
7	Aftermath	82
8	A Strange Kind of Triumph	94
9	The Debacle of 1954	103
10	Italian Interlude	118
11	Coventry City	125
12	The Low Point at Highfield Road	135
13	Back to Sweden	147
14	The 1958 World Cup	159
15	Home at Last	172
16	The Most Important Book in English Football History	178
17	Dispute	195
18	The Descent	205
	Afterword	213
	Bibliography	222

ABOUT
THE AUTHOR

Ashley Hyne is a barrister and works in the north-west of England. A former football referee, he officiated in over 1,000 matches between 1996 and 2010 in Australia, New Zealand and Indonesia as well as in England. His interest in George Raynor stems from a conversation with Brian Glanville in the early 1980s, when Glanville erroneously informed him that Raynor 'had been dead for years'. Ashley is currently working on his next book which charts the life of Jesse Carver.

ACKNOWLEDGEMENTS

Thanks are due to the following who kindly assisted with information: Sid Raynor; Elsecar Heritage Centre; Paul Taylor and Martin Shaw, historians, Mansfield Town FC; Laura Orridge, Rotherham United FC; Jack Rollin; Royal Army Physical Training Corps museum; Bengt Agren; Sven Axbom; Bengt Berndtsson; Kurt & Marianne Hamrin; Hans Moller; Kalle Palmer; Bengt & Birgit Gustavsson; John Eriksson; Jim Brown; Lol Harvey; Jesper Zenk; Mick French; John Fennell; George Crawford; Lawrie McMenemy; Roy Hodgson; Gordon Pulley; Guy Mowbray; Alan Bates; Vivienne Ashworth; Lina Hedvist; Neil Bonnan; David Magilton; Michael Joyce; Laura Niland; Andrew Kirkham; Denis Clarbrough; Stephen Fay; Dan Fells; Allan Wills; Tommy Wahlsten; Gordon Small; Brian Hyde; Hassanin Mubarak; Anders Johren. Thanks to Karen Bush without whom this book would not have been possible.

FOREWORD BY
GORDON PULLEY

Gordon Pulley was a professional footballer who played on the right-wing for Millwall, Gillingham and Peterborough in the Football League after a brief stint with non-league Oswestry Town. His playing career lasted from 1956 to 1966. In total, Gordon played 282 league matches and scored 58 league goals, including a rather controversial goal in a game at Coventry City when George Raynor was seated in the home dugout. Following his playing career, Gordon was a sports teacher at schools and colleges in south London. This foreword will give the reader a taste of what the game was like during the 1950s when Raynor came back to work in England from Sweden.

~

My own introduction to being a professional footballer in the 1950s started when I was doing National Service in the army while I was stationed at Oswestry. After an army game I was asked by Alan Ball Snr (the Oswestry Town FC manager) if I would join his club for £4 per week. After playing only 4 games for the club, I was transferred to Millwall, signing for the club on 17 September 1956 and made my debut at Watford the evening after.

My salary at that time was restricted to £8 per week due to my being on National Service. Having to travel from Oswestry army camp for every game proved to be tiring. Playing in a home game at The Den would see me leave the camp on a Friday evening, stay overnight at my home in the West Midlands and continue to London on the Saturday morning, usually arriving at the ground at approximately 2 p.m. and then returning back home at 10 a.m. A long day for a home game!

The away games were even more difficult. For the away games I had to be in London quite early on the Saturday morning to meet up with the team, which meant staying on Friday night at the Union Jack Club, which was a hostel for the Armed Forces, and I usually arrived back home around midnight and got back to camp on Sunday. On one occasion, due to bad weather, I arrived late at The Den for a home game just as the players were leaving the dressing room, with a player being put in my place, but he was stopped from entering the field, so that I could take my usual place in the team. The game had been going for about 10 minutes before I got on to the field. I still had seven months to go before I left the army, so every weekend followed the same schedule.

There were many professional players stationed at Oswestry at the time, and I imagine that they all had similar travel problems. My first season at Millwall went reasonably well, considering that I was trying to come to terms with my first taste of League football, which I found to be a lot more physical than playing non-league, and also to compete against full-time players whilst still being in the army. I felt that sometimes the management didn't always appreciate this.

My first season was notable for a good FA Cup run, which saw victories against Brighton, Margate, Crystal Palace and Newcastle United before losing to Birmingham City in the fifth round. Both the Newcastle and Birmingham games attracted gates of 40,000 for both home games at The Den. I well remember defeating Brighton in a replay in an evening game at The Den, because when I reported back to camp the following morning I spent the day locked up in the Guard Room for being absent without leave: the club had forgotten to contact the regiment to arrange for me to have the Monday off.

The Den could be an intimidating ground to play on, and not only for the away side. The home fans would never shy away from letting you know how they felt about your display. It was sometimes very wise to leave the ground long after the fans had gone. Later on, in the early Gillingham days, I would travel by bus to the home games together with quite a few of the fans who lived near to me. The result decided whether we came back on the same bus.

On leaving the army for my first full-time contract with the club, I received a salary of £14 in the first team, plus a win bonus of £4, £11 in the reserves and £8 in the summer. This improved in time to £17, £14 and £11 in the summer. Being a professional footballer in the 1950s was a vastly different proposition to that of today in so many ways. There was no security of long-term contracts. The contracts were for one year only and at the end of each playing season you would receive (by registered mail) the decision of the club. There were three choices open to them: either to retain your services for a further year (usually on the same salary), to give you a free transfer or, the worst of all for a player, to place you on the 'open to transfer' list. Being placed on the open to transfer list meant that the club would put a fee on your head, but if no other club had bought you by the time your contract had ended at the end of May (which was only a few short weeks after the season had ended) the club ceased not only to play you, but also retained your resignation, so you were not able to move to another club until someone wanted to pay the fee that they were asking for.

Over a period of time the club could either reduce the fee required, or grant a free transfer to the player in order for him to move on. Either way the player would have been seriously out of pocket, not to mention the stress it would have caused before he finally moved to a club. So in theory you were at that time out of football and at the mercy of the directors. No club, no salary and it was quite legal for football clubs to do this. I was fortunate that my transfer to Gillingham from Millwall went through before my contract had ended. Jimmy Hill was later to call this 'Soccer Slavery', which was a good description.

On the playing side, the usual formation of the teams was 3–2–2–3: three defenders, two wing halves, two inside forwards and three front players. The two wing halves would normally support the back three and the two inside forwards would play just behind the front three. With the odd exception, most playing surfaces in those days in the lower divisions were not that good, particularly after Christmas when you were all too often playing on a pitch of sand and mud. Football in the Third Division South and the 4th Divisions tended to be quite physical, but in the 1950s, football was known to be a contact sport, and although most of the defenders were tough and uncompromising in their approach to the game, very few of them found their way in to the referees' book, no matter how bad the tackles were. I can only remember one opposing player ever being sent off the field in a game that I played in. That was against Bradford Park Avenue, when the then player-manager of Bradford, the legendary tough Ronnie Scoular (formerly of Newcastle United and Scotland fame) grabbed one of the Gillingham players by the throat. It took something extreme to get your marching orders in those days. Certainly a few bad tackles from behind would never get a player in too much trouble: in the 1950s the tackle from behind was quite acceptable to the referees if not to the player on the receiving end.

Although the game was very physical there were very few penalties awarded. I was designated penalty taker for quite a few seasons, but can only remember taking approximately six and they were usually given for hand ball. Although the 3rd and 4th Divisions were well known for their physical approach, there was no real cheating, no shirt pulling, no trying to get an opponent sent off, and for all the tough tackles that were made, it was mainly an honest game. When I was on the receiving end of a strong challenge my first thought was to get to my feet and try to walk away and to show the full-back that he hadn't hurt me. Not always easy, but most wingers I played with would all do the same. We didn't want to show the defender that he could kick you out of the game. Our manager would always tell our full-backs that when the winger is trying to take you on, the ball can go past you, the winger can go past you, but not the two together. You have to get one or the other. It appeared to me that nearly all the opposing full-backs in the 1950s used to receive this same advice. When scoring a goal, you might get a pat on the back, a handshake or a well done from a teammate but no more than that.

The goalkeepers were certainly not a protected species in the 1950s. Many a goal was scored with the goalkeeper lying injured on the ground after being challenged by an opponent when attempting to catch a high cross. I well remember one controversial incident when I played in a game for Millwall against Coventry City at Highfield Road in 1956. The Coventry goalkeeper that day was Reg Matthews, who was at that time an England international. He came out to catch a high ball from a right-wing corner and after a strong challenge from a couple of Millwall players he couldn't hang on to the ball and fell injured to the ground, the ball fell invitingly to my feet which I promptly put into the empty goal. The game was held up for some time, not only to enable Reg to get treatment but due to the Coventry players disputing my goal and also to clear the pitch, after seat pads from the main stand had come raining down over the touchline from irate home fans. My goal was allowed to stand, and we went on to win the game 2–1.

Reg Matthews was later to join Chelsea, and when Chelsea and Millwall played home games on the same Saturdays we would sometimes have a meal together on the train back to the Midlands and to the best of my knowledge the controversial goal was never mentioned.

From my own time of football in the 1950s the two clubs I played for were run by the manager and a trainer who also doubled up as the physio. Most of the training sessions would be

lots of running, with laps around the pitch: the main emphasis
was on fitness, and very little was seen of the ball. A popular
belief in those days from the management was that if you didn't
see much of the ball during the week's training you would
want it more in the games. This was not the view of the players.
The only time spent with a ball, apart from the routine Tuesday
practice game, was normally to give the goalkeeper some
shooting practice and when we organised our own small-sided
games on a rough patch of ground behind the terracing. It was
only when coaching became more acceptable in time, that the
ball skills practices came into their own and the sessions became
more enjoyable.

Training was almost always held at the ground, and a lot of it
on the pitch, usually in all weathers, which is why the playing
surface in the latter part of the season was difficult to play on.
It was not unusual to see a very heavy roller used on a Friday to
flatten the playing surface.

There weren't a series of pre-season friendlies in those days:
on the Saturday before the season started, there would be a
game between the First Team and the Reserves, and that's all.
One season there were only sixteen professionals at the club
and five young professionals who were known as ground staff
boys, who besides training to be footballers had to do jobs
around the ground. When we had a practice match on a Tuesday
the manager, Harry Barratt, would often join in to even the
teams up. The training kit tended to be several years old and
the first arrivals would get the best kit. In many ways Harry
could be described as a pre-Brian Clough type of manager,
he was a tough competitor during his playing days for Coventry,
and he managed in the same way, with a real sense of humour at
times. He often used to say to me that he couldn't understand
why I could play so well in one game and so bad the next.
He even got his mentor and the former Coventry City manager,
Harry Storer, to come and watch our game at Notts Forest, for
advice on how to get the best out of me. His favourite comment
to me after many a game was 'You started off bad, and got worse.'

The relationship with a manager tended to depend on whether you were in the first team, playing well, and winning games. When that happened everything was fine but when you were left out of the team, things changed. You were rarely told the bad news by the manager although you would have had a good idea in the week's training. You only really found out what team you were playing in when the team sheets were pinned on the notice board on a Friday morning and when you were left out of the side – which could be for quite a few weeks – there was usually little contact between the manager and the player, hardly any conversations at all, and you were ignored until you were put back into the side and things improved again.

On one occasion when I was left out of the Gillingham team and not too happy, I followed the advice of several senior professionals. They encouraged me to go and see the manager, Harry Barratt (which I foolishly did), to ask him why I was playing in the second team on the Saturday, to which he replied in a rather loud voice, 'Because we haven't got a third team for you to play in,' and promptly tore me to pieces. I returned to a dressing room full of laughter, as the players had heard every word that was said. What a set up.

But I didn't fare as badly as one of Gills' players, Brian Payne, who was involved in a confrontation with Harry Barratt. After an evening reserve game at Crystal Palace, which ended in a heavy defeat, all the team were ordered to report for training next morning. In the team meeting the next morning they were told to expect a hard session of running as punishment for the previous night's poor display. Barratt said, 'And if anyone objects and doesn't want to do the running, then say so now and you can have a week's wages and leave the club.' Brian didn't agree with the manager's decision, said so and within minutes was out of football and didn't play league football again. It was quite a usual thing at the time when after a bad defeat, the manager would nearly always vent his anger by ordering the trainer to make the players suffer: the reasons why or how we came to lose a game were never exactly explained – it was always too often

that 'the effort was lacking' and 'we hadn't tried hard enough'
and very little analysis was used to say what we had done wrong,
whether individually or as a team. This was also to change when
coaches became more involved in the teams.

Life in the Fourth Division could be quite tough
travelling-wise, especially for an evening away game when
playing against a Northern club. Money was tight and it meant
travelling by coach on most occasions, which meant spending all
day on a coach and travelling back through the night after the
game. At Gillingham we had quite a problem with some of the
away fixtures. At an evening game at Barrow in late September
or early October, we missed the morning Euston train to the
North. It was an early kick-off because they had no floodlights
and as there was no other train that would get us there in time
for the game, it was decided to go to Heathrow and try to
hire a plane. It was a worrying time for the officials, because
no club had ever failed to arrive for a Football League fixture.
After several hours a plane was hired and we flew to Blackpool
which was still quite some distance from Barrow. A fleet of taxis
completed the journey. The kick-off was delayed for some time,
but after approximately 1 hour's play and being 6 or 7–0 down it
was just too dark to complete the game.

It was the first Football League fixture at that time where the
game was abandoned and the result was allowed to stand. And to
complete a miserable day, we travelled back overnight on a train.
The club received only a nominal fine, because of the high cost
of hiring a plane. Further away trips to Walsall, where we arrived
with only eight players (the other three had missed the train,
although they arrived in time for the game), and to Doncaster
and Workington also saw us arrive only just in time to make the
kick-off. For the Doncaster game we were travelling by train and
were preparing to get off when approaching Doncaster station,
only to be told that the train was not scheduled to stop there,
and the communication cord had to be pulled by one of our
officials. The train came to a halt beyond the station which meant
a walk back along the track before taking taxis to the ground.

For the Workington game we had to get changed on the coach and only just made the kick-off once again. Life was never dull on the road with the Gills. Sometimes the coach trips back to Kent from the North could also be difficult after a bad result. Geoff the driver, who also doubled up as the groundsman, was told by the manager that we would be travelling back without any stops unless the manager wanted to stop for the toilet, when the players could do the same: but a good result away from home would see us make several stops at various pubs along the way.

The holiday period was a busy time in the 1950s with games on both Christmas Day and Boxing Day, while over the Easter weekend we would play on Good Friday, Saturday and the Monday. As a footballer in the 1950s we didn't earn much more than the average worker would have earned and we possibly earned less during the summer: the close season saw most of the players looking for a job to supplement the low summer wage. In the 1950s the summer break was approximately ten weeks long. I did various jobs over quite a few summers, such as working in a timber yard, a labourer and I was once employed by Gillingham with other players to paint the dressing rooms and do odd jobs around the ground. Other times, with my wife and two young girls, we would spend the whole summer back home in the West Midlands, where we both came from, dividing our time between our parent's homes.

I married my wife Pat during my early days at Millwall, but the only way I could get manager Ron Gray's permission to get married during the season was to marry in the morning in the Midlands, and play at Coventry in the afternoon, which we did. All the married players at that time would rent houses owned by the club, with the single players living in digs. One football kit would have to last the whole season, and on one occasion when the club played in the FA Cup away at Ashford Town (Kent) and the strips clashed we had to borrow a kit from Margate FC for the game.

We even had to buy our own boots. A pair of new football boots in the 1950s usually had to be broken in before you would want to play a game in them. I would remove the studs, soak the boots in warm water for some time, and after drying them off, would wear them around the house for days until they felt comfortable enough to use for the first time. Two pairs of boots would last me a whole season, one with studs for the soft pitches, and one with moulded rubber studs for when they were firm. When they did wear out, I had to get them repaired myself.

An injury could also cause you real financial problems, because if you got injured playing for the first team and were out of action for quite some time, you would only receive first-team wages for the next four weeks. You would then receive reserve-team money until you were fit and back in the side. This never seemed fair to me, almost like adding insult to injury.

But to be a footballer in the 1950s and 1960s was all that I wanted to be. As players we never thought we were anything special just because we played football, particularly playing in the lower divisions. I always considered myself very much a working-class person who was grateful to be earning a salary doing something that I really enjoyed and of the opinion that it was better than having to work for a living. I had no other plans and looking back it would have been nice to have had the security of a longer contract, better pitches to play on, also a little more protection from the officials, but nevertheless, to be able to earn your living from kicking a ball around took some beating.

Gordon Pulley, 2013

INTRODUCTION

Despite being the most successful national coach in the history of football – an accolade bestowed by the *Guinness Book of Records* – Raynor is one of the least well known within Great Britain. Rising from humble beginnings as a miner's son, he became a competent but unexceptional footballer for Second and Third Division clubs before discovering his real forte and beginning a meteoric ascent as a coach.

Dispatched to Sweden after the Second World War, Raynor achieved such success at international level that he clearly came to believe, justifiably, that he would one day be given the responsibility to lead England. His work overseas therefore carries with it the feeling that all was a rehearsal for a triumphant return. However, this was never to come to pass. In this way, Raynor, although an ambassador for English football, became increasingly a reluctant and embittered one.

Against all the odds, he steered Sweden to Olympic Gold and Bronze medals as well as to second and third places in two World Cups, and managed Italian giants Lazio and Juventus. Yet on leaving Sweden in 1958, the man whose services had been recognised with a knighthood from the King of Sweden and a Presidential Medal from the Brazilian Government was inexplicably (or widely presumed to be) shunned by First Division clubs and found himself working at a grammar school in Skegness as a PE teacher.

In his own country George Raynor was, and continues to be, ignored or misunderstood. His successes were received by sceptics and resisted by those who had no genuine interest in seeing England win anything. Even today references to him in football history books are disparaging: 'A little known clogger,' according to one, and in another (a history of football tactics no less) reference to Raynor is not only fleeting but his name misspelt. Jonathan Wilson's binning of Raynor's impact on the ascendance of Swedish football (and, indeed, European football after the Second World War in general) in his *Inverting the Pyramid* is astonishing not least in its brevity: 'Under [Raynor's] guidance, and advantaged by their wartime neutrality, Sweden won Gold at the 1948 London Olympics, finished third at the 1950 World Cup and then reached the final against [Brazil] in 1958. There, they played a typical WM with man-marking ...' And that's it!

Did Sweden really play 'a typical WM' formation? If they did so play, how could such an antiquated formation produce such success? And, given that it was successful, what influence, if any, did Sweden's play have on other nations? Moreover, how much a factor was the Swedish neutrality in the war? Particularly in light of the comparative lack of success of Switzerland and Spain who, equally, were neutral in the war.

Is this commonplace ignorance and disdain for Raynor's achievements an indication that Olympic Gold in 1948 and Bronze in 1952, and a second and third place in the 1958 and 1950 World Cup were commonplace and that his ideas lacked tactical sophistication? Is it evidence that the 7–2 victory over Karl Rappan's Switzerland in 1946 and a 2–2 draw with Gustav Sebes' world-beating Hungarians in November 1953 – just days before Hungary beat England 6–3 – were merely the results of luck and chance? Under Raynor's tutelage, at each and every international competition in which Sweden qualified they 'medalled'. Yet in England, the nation which yearned so much for a victory their self-belief should have confirmed, there was never a desire to bring Raynor into the fold. He was quite possibly the greatest coach England never had.

George Raynor's story might ostensibly be regarded as just another straightforward 'poor boy makes good' tale, but in fact it is one which, when examined more closely, raises a number of intriguing questions. Apart from the obvious – why his methods were so outstandingly successful – probably the most perplexing and difficult to answer is why his evident talents and experience were never to be called upon by his own country. The purpose of this book is to attempt to answer these questions by examining Raynor's career in football.

Ashley Hyne, 2014

1

THE EARLY
YEARS

Knowing a little about Raynor's background is instructive, as the part played by the environment and circumstances he grew up in sheds light on the formative influences on his character which would ultimately lead to some of his greatest successes – and later, his bitterest disappointments.

One of four children, George Raynor was born in Elizabeth Street, Hoyland, South Yorkshire, on 13 January 1907. The Raynors lived and grew up in an area dominated by coal mines; George's father Fred worked as a coal hewer, as did his grandfather, another George. From the age of 16, George's uncle Wilfred also worked underground, as a coal trammer, a job which involved pulling and pushing the pony-pulled trams to the surface of the pit. George Raynor had no inclination to follow them into the dirt and blackness. He should not be criticised for not wishing to do so. Pit work was frightening, dangerous, and bloody hard work.

Charlie Williams, who would later find fame on TV's *The Comedians*, was a miner before becoming a professional footballer and was, himself, coached by Raynor while playing for Skegness Town in the 1960s. Williams wrote briefly about the reality of pit work in his autobiography *Ee – I've had some laughs*:

> The first coal face I saw were the Barnsley Seam. It were five, maybe six, feet high. You could stand up in that one. I've seen colliers in smaller seams when they've had to kneel to get at the coal. And there were sparks flying off them picks. Hand-got coal. No machines then. Hand-got. The colliers picked it down, then they shovelled it. Graft. Them men worked. They deserved every penny they got.

Williams devotes just as much time to discussing the misery experienced by the pit ponies as he does to the miners. This is not accidental, either. The ponies were an integral part of a system that bonded that community, and when Williams writes about the death of ponies – invariably due to the carelessness of some absent-minded trammer leaving a shaft door unlatched – it is not just out of sympathy for the animals but because death was always somewhere close in that darkness.

Nowadays we think of the unity of the mine workers as being implicitly political in nature, but that affiliation arose because of the system the miners worked in. Each miner was dependent on their fellow workers for their survival. This sense of unity would not have been lost on the young George Raynor. He came from a small mining village in South Yorkshire and that same unity bound the community. Power, strength and survival all came from people working together for the common good. Later in life, when he lived and worked in Sweden, Raynor would demonstrate just how creating that same unity of purpose would come as second nature to him and how it would benefit those he worked with.

George excelled academically from an early age. By the end of the First World War the family had moved to No. 6 Hall Street, Hoyland, and at that time Raynor was attending Hoyland Combined School. In his autobiography *Football Ambassador at Large*, Raynor recounts that he was in Standard 7 at the age of 10 and in August 1919 he was awarded a County Minor scholarship from the West Riding County Council to attend Barnsley and District Holgate Grammar School, which later became Barnsley Grammar School. This would be the school of footballers Brian and Jimmy Greenhoff, and of cricket umpire Dickie Bird.

The scholarship was not, however, the blessing it might have been. Another student of the school, chat show host Michael Parkinson, later bitterly referred to the place in anything but glowing terms: 'Barnsley Grammar School was to education what myxomatosis was to rabbits.'

Raynor would attend the school as a day boarder from the age of 12 in September 1919 until he was 15 in July 1922. Raynor's experience of school life was summed up by one incident that he recounted in his autobiography. During a PE class, Captain Henry McNab Bisley, an ex-army school teacher who was taking the lesson, smacked Raynor across the ear for turning up in his vest and underpants – an 'outfit' which speaks of the relative deprivation in which Raynor grew up.

Although Raynor was to remark that as a result of that incident he recoiled from physical training, this is not true. George was in fact a self-taught and talented athlete and used his autobiography to explain how he loved sports, and trained himself in athletics.

What Raynor did learn from the incident was that he would never become the same sort of small-minded sadist that Bisley arguably was. He had no time for the type of authoritarians that used sport as an excuse to bully their charges. In his later career, Raynor would assume the role of pastoral carer for his charges, the very antithesis of all that Bisley represented. Raynor's coaching methods demonstrated conclusively that the reward of proper, supportive tutoring was the flourishing of ability where talent might otherwise have remained inhibited. Over eighty years after Bisley's life-changing slap, Kurt Hamrin, the wing-star of Sweden in the 1950s, wrote warmly of the type of coach that George Raynor became, saying, 'He was an incredibly nice man, we lads in the [Swedish national] team referred to him as *finagubben*' – which is difficult to translate, but is basically a respectful but familiar nickname equivalent to something like 'the grand gaffer'.

One cannot know what discussions took place at the Raynor family home before and after George left school about what direction his life should take, but we can be fairly sure that the heartfelt desire of George's family was not to join the queue into the pit. Forced to leave school at the age of 15 when his father lost his job in 1922, Raynor got an apprenticeship in a local butchery. It was not a sinecure, being often bloody and violent (one of George's tasks was to kill pigs by hammering a peg between their eyes) but the job, which to modern eyes hardly represents a vindication of a renowned education, would have definitely represented upward social mobility in a mining town.

Hasties, the company George gained the apprenticeship with, were an established local company and one can reasonably believe that the family would have been content with the appointment. However, George's mind was on participating in sport. He was clearly a talented athlete from an early age, and it was because of his early love of participation and competition that George himself brought the apprenticeship to an end. One of the first indications of his leanings toward sport and away from a normal working life came about one Saturday. George was granted time off to race in the local sprint handicap at Platts Common, just north of Hoyland. He won the race. Then returned, exhilarated, to work and finished his shift.

Irked by the fact that working at Hasties was occupying him on Saturday, 'the day of sport', George handed in his notice and went to work as a labourer on a builder's lorry instead. This was physically demanding and tiring work but there were benefits to be gained from it. He took the job because, in his mind, it would help strengthen him as he matured through his teens – and most importantly of all, it left him free on Saturdays. As Raynor's cousin Sid, who still lives in Hoyland, wryly comments, 'He never really did do a proper job, you know.'

Around this time George decided that he wanted to be a professional footballer.

Number 6 Hall Street still exists today, part of the town square of Hoyland; one of a row of terraced houses which face onto a car park. Turning left out of his front door, Raynor would free-wheel his push bike halfway down King Street, and in a side alley next to the tennis and bowling green (where the access road to the Park and Ride is now found) he would devote time to sprint training. It was also there that he would meet his future wife, Phyllis Whitfield.

Phyllis lived at No. 97 Church Street, Elsecar almost next door to the Wesleyan Chapel. She was a member of a Bible Class which was run at the chapel. She knew George liked football and explained to George that the Bible Class had a football team and that if George wanted to play football he could do so on condition that he joined the Bible Class. This George proceeded to do.

The minister running the Bible Class was Thomas Tomlinson. This was the beginning of a life-long friendship between George and Thomas and was George's introduction into organised football.

The Bible Class played on Furnace Hills in Elsecar. The area still exists, although it's now beneath 3ft of seeded grass and there are maturing trees dotted around what was the pitch. It can be found on a flat step of ground, on the hill above the Elsecar Heritage Centre; to access it one has to navigate a treacherous course up a muddy path.

It was a popular venue for the local football teams (Elsecar played their home matches there). Alan Crossley (uncle of Welsh international goalkeeper Mark), who I met at Furnace Hills, explained to me that it was used by the local school teams whose pupils would run from King Street School across King Street, along Church Street and all the way up the hill before playing a match and then running back to the school to get changed. But, as Alan said, it was never a grass pitch. Instead Furnace Hills was a dumping ground for the shale that was extracted out of the Elsecar Main Coal Pit, which is likely where George's father earned his crust.

The shale was dumped on the side of the pitch and this served as impromptu terracing where local spectators would gather to watch the games that were played at the ground.

The bumpy surface made it a difficult pitch to play, and the jagged rocks of shale frequently caused cuts and bruises. Later, in the 1980s, that same shale would be dug out of the soil by some members of the local community, who, impoverished by the extended miner's strike, were reduced to burning the discarded waste.

George played centre forward for the team in the Sunday School League and helped the club raise money for local charities when playing in the popular Kelley Cup, a local competition. Raynor would look back on those local youth games with great fondness. Half a century later, Raynor could still recall scoring 73 goals for Elsecar Bible Class in one season. Those 73 goals made an impression locally because Mexborough, one of the local Midland League sides, asked George to play in a trial.

The Midland League was a reserve league, featuring both football league reserve sides and some of the best non-league teams in that part of the country and had become a scouting ground for various local football league sides. George jumped at the chance of attending the trial. Only 20 minutes from Elsecar, Mexborough had won the Midland League in the 1925/26 season and during the following season won their way into the first round of the FA Cup, only to lose narrowly to Chesterfield of the Football League.

This contemporary success probably explains why Mexborough did not contact young Raynor following the trial match, despite him scoring twice. It is also a reasonable assumption that Mexborough did not really take to Raynor because he wasn't the big, bustling centre forward that the Midland League demanded; even when fully grown Raynor was only 5ft 7in in height and 11 stone in weight.

However, it wasn't long before George had a chance in another trial match; this time for Wombwell, another Midland League side. This time he was more successful and, in July 1929, he signed forms to play for Wombwell for 15s per match. The first decision Wombwell's management made on signing Raynor was to assess his lack of height, note his speed and place him on the right-wing, a position he would remain in for the rest of his career.

Raynor had a splendid debut for Wombwell, shining in a game against the leaders of the Midland League, Notts County reserves. It was also during that game that an incident occurred which made a deep impression on George, and would later influence the way he coached his players. He describes scoring a goal: 'I took one pass, raced around two men, took the ball up to the byline and surprised the goalkeeper with a tremendous shot from that almost impossible angle.' As Raynor gleefully headed back to the halfway line, the side's resident professional and captain, Denis Jones (formerly with Leicester City), went up to Raynor and instead of offering congratulations, gave him a short, sharp comment to the effect that he should never do that again. The lesson was not lost on George. To succeed in football – particularly in the Midland League between the wars – required self-discipline and subservience to the team. Raynor was happy to defer to the experienced club professional, for his words were those of a person who had already been where Raynor wanted to go, and Jones' lesson was timeless: unnecessary risk should be avoided at all costs.

It was a lesson he would return to throughout his career, memorably so in one of the first games he saw played in Sweden. In a virtuoso display mirroring that of the young Raynor, a young inside right called Gunnar Gren beat three defenders, rounded the goalkeeper, took the ball back to beat the goalkeeper again and then back-heeled the ball over the line. Raynor brought Gren down to earth with a thud after the game with his imitation of a Denis Jones' style rocket.

Raynor's instruction that Gren must pass the ball away as soon as he had beaten his opponent led to a falling out between the two. Gren's battered pride would subside, a natural instinct to win for the team soon undermining his initial response that he would rather kick the ball into touch than pass, and in Raynor's words he became one of the finest team-men you could wish to find. Raynor was never unnecessarily harsh on his players, who responded accordingly. He had never forgotten Jones' lesson that 'For any player to shoot from the by-line is the height of selfishness, and although he might score once in a hundred times, his selfishness costs his team a goal on most of the other occasions. There is no room in football for the selfish player, the player who puts the glory of scoring a goal above the good of the team.'

Raynor's performances on the right-wing for Wombwell soon put him in the shop window for some of the local

Football League sides. In one of his games, knowing that United's scout was watching, Raynor played despite having torn a calf muscle shortly before the game; typically undeterred, he played through the game with a heavily strapped leg. The future looked bright when, on 18 May 1930, he signed professional forms for First Division Sheffield United. Just a few weeks earlier George Raynor's life had changed in a completely different way and, on 3 May, he had married Phyllis Whitfield at the Wesleyan Chapel where they both attended the Bible Class as children; the lay preacher who married them was Tommy Tomlinson.

2

A PLAYING CAREER
UNFULFILLED?

There is a celebrated story about Raynor's first meeting with Jimmy Dunne, the Irish international and captain of Sheffield United in the early 1930s. The Irishman asked Raynor where he was from. 'Hoyland' replied Raynor in his Yorkshire accent. 'Put it there, if it weighs a ton!' said Dunne, believing Raynor was from Ireland and thrusting out a hand in welcome.

Upon such a misunderstanding Raynor embarked on his Football League career: it was also to prove one of the few light-hearted moments during it. After signing for Sheffield United, George's stay was brief and without glory. Indeed, most of his early Football League career was unpromising and the fact that he stuck with it demonstrates his colossal enthusiasm and unbridled self-belief – a less resolute man might well have admitted defeat, particularly given the financial commitment he now had to his young family. Raynor was later to write: 'When you have to do a thing you will drive yourself forward and do it in the face of all difficulties, instead of sitting down and throwing in the towel.' Although referring to his wartime experiences, it was a philosophy he'd already learned to apply to his earlier career and was to be a constant characteristic throughout his life.

At the time, United were a team in trouble; their long-serving coach, George Waller, had retired in 1930, and at the end of the 1929/30 season they scraped themselves away from relegation. Raynor made no league appearances at all for the Blades during the first season he was with them; a season during which the only cheer for him was at home, when in February 1931 Phyllis gave birth to their first son, Brian. When Raynor did turn out for the first team (in the local County FA Cup tie on 31 October 1931) it was hardly a memorable occasion.

United lost 4–1.

To Sheffield Wednesday.

One reason for his lack of appearances was that the club had five wingers on the books at the time. Sid Raynor recalls George's conversations with Sid's father about the wing partnerships (those between the outside and inside rights) at Sheffield United that had been formed before George's arrival. According to Sid, inside forwards would deliberately cut Raynor out of the game, starving him of the ball so that their preferred wing partner would be retained. George Raynor was discovering that professional football was about playing the game in the dressing room as well as on the park; maybe his youth or his lone character worked against him, or perhaps it was his outspokenness which didn't go down well.

Whatever the reason for his inability to break into those partnerships, George would talk to his Uncle Wilfred of the bizarre loneliness of pacing up and down the grassy expanse of the right-wing at Bramall Lane in the pre-season summer sun without reward or service. In those days, half of the field was an unused cricket pitch – United shared the stadium with Yorkshire CCC – and the ground had three stands for the football pitch, and one touchline would back on to the expanse of the cricket field.

These were worrying times for Raynor, unable to break out of the reserves and gain a foothold in the first team. The one bright spot for him at that time was meeting Harry Johnson, the reserve team trainer at Bramall Lane, who instilled a set of

down-to-earth values that Raynor welcomed and would duly
refer back to in time:

Never let your skill in football make you big-headed, or make
you forget where and how you started.
Never allow a 'clogger' to bring you down to his level.
Keep off drink and train hard.

Sheffield United put Raynor on the transfer list at the end of
May 1932. At that time players were contracted on a year-by-year
basis, which meant that if you were transfer listed by a club in
May you would be surviving from hand to mouth during the
summer months with no guarantee of a club being interested
in your services come the next season. In practice, clubs would
not sign new players before the summer break because it would
mean paying for staff who would not be required to work and as
Raynor later recalled, 'I was refused any dole because the Labour
Exchange claimed footballers were seasonal workers.'

Fortunately, Raynor was signed by Football League new-boys
Mansfield Town in time for the 1932/33 season. He took over
from the outside right Billy Cupit for the game at Barrow on
3 September 1932. A high scoring run of 6 games followed,
but Raynor (again) found it difficult securing a permanent
first-team spot, particularly when manager Jack Hickling
brought an experienced right-winger, Jack Prior, to the club.
In his autobiography George tried to put a positive spin on the
situation, but the reality was that after losing his spot to Prior he
would only ever be acting as second fiddle.

Raynor was recalled for a brief run of games when he played
3 consecutive matches between the middle of November and
early December 1932, but after that Prior remained immoveable.
Raynor did not want to yield to what Hickling was asking: that
he change from the type of flying winger like Cliff Bastin to one
who could run and take on opponents, as Jack Prior could.

This refusal could not have helped the team: Raynor's 'run'
of games for Mansfield involved a home loss to Gateshead,

a first-round defeat in the cup at Walsall (who would famously go on to defeat Arsenal that season) and a scoreless draw at home to Wrexham. Apart from one more match – another loss, this time at Carlisle – that would be that for Raynor at Mansfield Town. The 'failure' to succeed at Mansfield Town presumably came as a result of the impossibility of the request of Jack Hickling. With his short stature and light weight, Raynor simply wasn't built for the role that Hickling envisaged. It wasn't a lack of willingness to subsume his preferences so much as a physical inability to comply. Although Mansfield offered him a renewed contract for the 1933/34 season (wages of £208 for the season beginning in August 1933) because there was no offer of summer wages when there were hungry mouths to feed at home, Raynor decided to leave.

By May 1933, his league career had amounted to two professional clubs and 9 first-team matches in three years. Fearing that his career was at an end he asked a friend to loan him a lorry so that he could start a coal-bagging business and return to playing part-time. A reprieve materialised when in August 1933 Reg Freeman, the manager at Rotherham United, offered him the opportunity to play in a series of pre-season friendlies. It was later revealed to Raynor that a fair amount of interest in his performances had been expressed during those trials and this gave him the self-assurance to stay with football. Rotherham offered him terms, and a goal from Raynor on his debut, albeit in a 5–1 reverse at Chester, in the opening game of the 1933/34 season signalled brighter times ahead.

He quickly formed a useful partnership on the right-wing with Vic Wright, a free scoring inside right who was on his second spell with the club. However, Wright's 8 goals in 6 games in the early part of the season placed him firmly on the transfer radar, and in early March 1934 Liverpool put in an offer that was too good for Rotherham to refuse. Although George struggled in the scoring stakes during 1933/34 (6 goals only) he did help the club in a modest run in the FA Cup, grabbing a goal against Coventry City when he played despite not having fully recovered from a broken collarbone – his arm was strapped, painfully, to his side. Otherwise though, the season was a disaster at Millmoor; Rotherham finishing second from bottom of the Third Division (North).

It didn't look as though the situation could get much worse for Raynor, but it did. During the following season, noting over-confidence in George, Reg Freeman dropped him from the first team for a couple of weeks in November 1934. It was a tough but necessary lesson which gave George no alternative but to fight his way back into the favours of the club. When he returned he made his commitment clear with a brace of goals against Gateshead in early December 1934. He was forming another good partnership, this time with the hometown player Tom Fenoughty when Rotherham decided to cash in on Raynor in early February 1935.

Off he went to Bury in the Second Division for a fee of £1,000 (which was a considerable investment given his patchy career record at that time). George stated, in his biography, that this was the highest amount of money Bury had ever paid for a player. However, as statistician Gordon Small later pointed out, back in 1923 the club had purchased Peter Quinn for £1,125.

It was at Gigg Lane that George met Norman Bullock, a man way before his time, hidden away from historical scrutiny and never to receive the type of renown bestowed on his apparently more sophisticated contemporaries, and a man who would change Raynor's life.

Bullock was a radical, and in later years Raynor would refer to his time with Bury as being the starting point of some of the ideas that he was later to use as a coach.

Norman Bullock was the son of a middle-class cotton salesman, and his father's preferred career choice for his son was as a pharmacist. Bullock's family's wealth was apparent because when he first started playing football he did so as an amateur, although in the end he was persuaded to discard the white smock and put on Bury's white shirt when signing as a professional in 1920. Starting out as a centre forward, he was a member of the side that won promotion to the First Division in the 1923/24 season, which went on to finish 4th in the First Division in 1925/26 and won 4 representative caps, including 1 game against Belgium in 1923 and 1 for the Football League.

Bullock was what some might call a *thinking* footballer. Charles Buchan described him as 'a studious type of leader, not a battering ram but beating defenders by positional play'. That may be the case but in his heyday Bullock was quite the enthusiastic player. In the September 1953 edition of *Charles Buchan's Football Monthly*, Bullock wrote:

> I was not a centre forward in the classic mould, I was a glutton for work and always had an almost uncontrollable urge to get possession of the ball ... Most centre forwards [of the day] feared a tussle with Frank Barson, the old Aston Villa and Manchester United centre-half ... In the course of a game [possibly Manchester United v Bury during the 1925/26 season] he would grunt in my ear: 'Why don't you keep still? You're dragging me out of position all the time.'

In fact, it is apparent that Bullock's decision to play behind the line came about around the same time that Jimmy Seed was employing a similar tactic when playing for Spurs. The fact that this change came in the very season in which the new offside law was introduced was not coincidental. What is apparent is that players were suddenly having to adapt and improvise and in Bullock's case that adaptation would lead to a change in his strategic approach to positioning,

Therefore, anyone seeking evidence of the formation of the deep-lying centre forward (the position that Hidegkuti would use to such devastation against England barely two months after Bullock's article was published) would do well to re-read that passage. Within it is contained the germ of an idea that set Bullock thinking strategically and one which led to the development of Raynor's 'G-man', Hungary's defeat of English football and, arguably, the very development of modern football. Indeed, I would go further for the significance of the comment was very much in keeping with the post-war world; a place where young intellectuals like Bullock were challenging previous conventions.

Later, during the war, when manager of Chesterfield, Bullock would watch games, not from the dugout but up in the stands to get a better perspective on the match. Bullock's managerial mentality is exemplified in an incident involving Jimmy Bullions. Bullock once dropped this Scottish player, telling him 'You're running around the field like a schoolboy,' adding, 'Come and sit with me in the stand.' Bullions, embarrassed at being dropped, and unable to appreciate the opportunity he was being offered of gaining a tactical demonstration of what was asked of him, handed in his transfer request. But the story of Bullions, albeit unsuccessful in that instance, signified the way Bullock approached his job and can best be summed up by the following: 'Let me show you what I mean, instead of bawling unhelpfully at you.'

After his international heyday in the mid-1920s, Bullock found the goals increasingly hard to come by, so the club decided to drop him back from the forward line, and started to play him as the centre half. After the change in the Offside law in 1925, this position became tactically critical as clubs sought to follow the lead of Herbert Chapman's Arsenal in creating a defensive stopper. Becoming the centre half was the perfect position for Bullock to see everything: that is to enable him to assess not only the game he was playing in, but also the way the game was developing.

Raynor's first game for Bury was Bullock's last as a player: an away win at Fulham on 9 February 1935. George showed no nerves, and had an immediate impact on the game. The *Bury Times* report of the game commented that, with a quarter of an hour to go, he set up Blackmore's winner, with a pass from right-wing half David Jones being played through by Raynor, and Blackmore letting fly from 30 yards, 'the ball swerving well out of the reach of the goalkeeper'.

In those days it was the role of the club directors of Bury to decide on team selection and in the weeks following his move Raynor was paired with various inside forwards. It seemed that despite the considerable outlay for their new player, the directors had not the wit to work out what to do with him. When he first started playing for Bury he was paired at different times with Jimmy O'Rourke, Tom Bagley, Joe Patrick and Willie Chambers. Chambers had only been fitfully employed as an inside forward during the 1934/35 season, and the beginning of his partnership with Raynor was inauspicious: a miserable 2–1 home defeat in late March to Manchester United. Bury's solitary goal that day was actually an own goal, scored by Walter Winterbottom, later to become the first full-time England manager.

Raynor's career with Bury might have gone the way of his previous contracts had it not been for a decision taken by the club's directors in December 1935. Between November and December that year Bury were in a right mess, gaining only 3 points out of a possible 16, and hitting rock bottom during the Christmas break when they shipped 11 goals in 2 matches. Raynor was being sidelined as the club tried to find the right formation to improve the club's fortunes. As a result the directors called an extraordinary general meeting to clear the air.

Norman Bullock, presumably as a result of his seniority, had the ear of the directors and must have made some proposals which were accepted because as a result of the meeting the Board handed him full managerial control. Incredibly (at a time when club directors dominated decision making), Bullock would now have complete responsibility for scouting, recruitment, team selection, coaching and team formations.

His first decision was to drop his incumbent right-wing pair of Bagley and Patrick, and select outside right Raynor and inside right Chalmers for the New Year's Day game at Southampton.

Although the result was a 0–0 scoreline, it was a positive performance in which both Chalmers ('always using the ball to good effect') and Raynor ('some of his work in the first half suggested that when he has settled down he will help to add life to the attack') shone. Only a fine save by Southampton goalkeeper Billy Light and 2 disallowed goals prevented Chalmers from giving Bury full points.

In the next game (against Blackpool) Raynor and Chalmers again worked well in combination. Twice pegged back against the home side, Raynor's crosses were converted by Buttery in the first half and then, with 3 minutes to go, Chalmers put Raynor clear and 'sending the ball forward to Matthews, who had moved from the centre of the field' allowed the centre forward to grab the winner.

Bullock finally became the manager of Bury after Christmas 1935, at the same moment when British football was going through a period of introspection and this led directly to change, a change that could be seen with the attempted introduction of a national coaching scheme in the mid-1930s.

Arguably there were five strands that created this need for change. The first was the legacy of loss of a proportion of young men during the First World War; the second was the election of Stanley Rous as FA Secretary in 1934; third was the introduction of home matches against Continental opposition from the 1930/31 season; fourth was the rise of Arsenal under the management of Herbert Chapman; and fifth was the alteration of what was then Law 6 (the offside law) in 1925.

The consensus was that there had been a dramatic reduction in individual skill at all levels of the game and unless the country's footballers could be coached and tactics developed then the national sport would be facing a bleak future. The body of people who proposed this argument were (like Bullock) all academics (invariably ex-private school educated, university men) which was significant because their impact (seen most notably with the astonishing displays of the Corinthian sides at the turn of the century) had sadly waned since the height of their golden age at the turn of the century. K.R.G. Hunt, when assistant master of Highgate School, stated in his *First Steps in Association Football* in 1924: 'one must confess with regret that the players who "pick themselves" [for the national side] scarcely exist nowadays and this is due … to a levelling down.'

This body was led (if that is the right word) by Stanley Rous, himself a graduate of St Luke's College in Exeter and the

school master of Watford Grammar School. It was Rous' idea
to kick-start the FA's coaching scheme; an idea that came to
fruition following Rous' election to the office of FA Secretary
in 1934. Rous, as others, had been profoundly affected by the
visit and display of the Austrian national side in London in
December 1932 and planned to address the sudden concern that
English football was, in all honesty, if not behind some of the
Continental sides, then struggling to remain on a competitive
level with them. England's record against foreign opposition had
already come to an end following a strenuous overland journey
to a stifling Madrid in 1929. That could be explained away;
what could not be explained away was the British public seeing
league stars being given the runaround in a climate suited to
British footballers.

One of the individuals at the vanguard of the movement
was F.N.S. Creek. He, like others, had felt moved enough to
have written a coaching manual and had signed up to the
FA's coaching courses. Out of that came *Association Football*
(published in 1937) which is still a highly recommended,
indeed relevant, book to read for those thinking of coaching.
The book certainly would have come to the attention of
Norman Bullock at Bury. Creek's book does not only deal
with instruction as to how youngsters should actually kick
a ball (a skill recent coaching books strangely avoid) but also
reviews tactical formations and the state of the game now
that the offside law had brought about a revision as to how
teams were organised. Despite covering the WM formation,
Creek is just as eager to point out that the withdrawn forward
and the dual centre-forward plan (adopted by Luton Town,
winners of the Third Division South that year) were just
as effective.

The alteration of Law 6 had provided that there would be
reduction in the number of defenders from three to two for the
purposes of determining if a player was in an offside position.
So it came to pass that just as the legislators had removed a player
from the defence, so the clubs set about putting a defender back

there: hence the rise of the 'third back', a defender who 'sat' between the two full-backs.

The alteration in the law revolutionised the game for it induced clubs to consider teamwork for the first time. Before 1925 teamwork existed in a form that would be utterly alien to modern eyes. As Steve Bloomer wrote in 1906:'There is no doubt that our half-backs of today are more skilful ... than they used to be, for their purpose was, only a few years ago ... understood to be the mere breaking up of an attack, and little more.'The idea of a midfield supporting an attack and being the fulcrum of an attack would have been unfathomable. Positions, like positions in a class-ridden society, were strictly prescribed: a full-back did this; a half-back did that. Forwards were obliged to retreat back with an opposition attack and compete for the loose ball if their half-backs had broken up the attack.

'Forward play' moreover meant forwards linking with other forwards in what was called 'combination football'. In other words interlinking passing between the inside and outside right or inside forwards and the centre. Villa's winger Charlie Athersmith and inside right for Derby Steve Bloomer, or Bloomer and, the Corinthian, G.O. Smith would advance for England, inter-passing between themselves until one or other got within range of a strike at goal. Otherwise wingers were to be found dribbling to the corner flag and delivering a cross to the centre of the area.

It was only with the alteration of the offside law and the way Arsenal successfully adapted to the change that one could see the development of the type of interlinking between the defence, midfield and attack that would be familiar to us now. Such was Arsenal's success that others sought to replicate the successful Arsenal 'system of play'. The man responsible for the success that Arsenal enjoyed was their late manager Herbert Chapman.

Chapman was hardly a revolutionary in realising that the change in the offside law required the need for an extra defender; a third back playing in a central role. Where Chapman differed from other coaches was in successfully linking the defence with the forwards, and by doing this masked the loss of a forward from the front line and, more importantly, ascribed roles to players to suit the system to such an effect that deficiencies could be masked.

The player Arsenal ultimately found to link the halves with the attack was Alex James who, though an inside forward, could be found as far back as his own area, picking up the ball from the third back, dribbling his way expertly out of trouble and, on a carved-up field, kicking a sodden leather ball 70 yards to the toes of Joe Hulme on the right-wing or Cliff Bastin on the left-wing (little wonder that in Bernard Joy's *Soccer Tactics* he presents a diagram of such a movement and entitles it 'the move that changed football').

Not only was James highly skilled in being able to pass short or long with accuracy and speed, but when he was in his own defensive third he had the vision and confidence to work his way out of trouble and instantly convert defence to attack.

However, Alex James was unique.

Creek wrote: 'It was, perhaps, only natural that, where one club had succeeded, others should follow … in a comparatively short time the vast majority of clubs in the country, down to the most humble of amateur sides, was playing the third back game. Yet it is doubtful if one in a hundred had the necessary talent to carry out the essential features of [Chapman's] plan.'

It was not simply the skill of the personnel which made Arsenal special. In Herbert Chapman, Arsenal had a manager with the foresight to apply intellect to give his side any advantage. One way Chapman did this was to encourage all playing staff to participate in 'team talks'. The novelty of this can be seen in the following anecdote. In *A Lifetime in Football* Charlie Buchan, a seasoned professional player, remembered an occasion at Arsenal when Dan Lewis, the normally quiet Arsenal goalkeeper, spoke up at a meeting of the players and argued that the full-backs should, when taking a throw near the corner, send it back to Lewis who would pass it on to the other back to thus start another attack. The fact that Buchan felt this incident was noteworthy highlights the novelty of team talks at that time.

What Norman Bullock brought to Bury was a rather novel approach at copying the Arsenal method. Bullock accepted that Bury simply did not have the personnel to replicate the Arsenal way, so instead he sought to utilise Bury's limited strengths.

Bullock considered that short passing was the best way out of the defensive third of the field, and decided that the best formation to achieve this was 3–3–4; that is a third back and (referring back to his own playing days) a withdrawn forward. This formation, according to F.N.S. Creek, had two benefits: the first was that the centre forward would drop back to pick up passes from the half-backs (as a result the opposing centre half would be lured out of his defensive position in search of the opposing centre forward, and Bury could exploit the gap vacated by the central defender); the second benefit was that the withdrawn centre forward filled a defensive function, filling the area between the centre half and the centre forward in the formation, adding defensive strength to the team.

One interesting point that Creek alludes to in his book is in relation to the way attacks actually developed. As Creek noted, teams may well line up with five forwards, but that did not necessarily mean that all five would attack. Teams may attack with one winger, a centre forward and an inside or outside forward since inside forwards were most likely to be disinclined to carry out fruitless advances up the field if the chances were that the centre forward would be the focus of the attack.

On that basis if there was third back and a withdrawn forward then if Bury, for instance, were lining up with four forwards only then in essence that could have been a 3–4–3 formation in the mid-1930s.

To compensate for the absence of the centre forward in the front line, Bullock would play the two inside forwards closer together, and keep his wingers wide. The centre forward would therefore link up with the halves who would make the short pass after tackling the opposing winger, and then the centre forward would pick up the short pass from the halves, advance up field and send a pass out to the wing to set the attack in motion.

Evidence that Bullock played four up front on first taking over management of Bury is provided by the match report of the game between Bury and Doncaster Rovers, published in the *Bury Times* of 29 January 1936, which stated: 'Like their opponents, Bury played with four forwards.' Clearly the players responded positively to the new formation introduced to them. They won 5–1 that day, with Raynor scoring his first goal for the club and setting up one goal with an impudent back heel.

The way in which Bullock set his team up to play might be viewed as a poor man's version of Chapman's plan, with short, quick passing to spring-board a counter-attack rather than 40–yard passes being sprayed out from defence; however, this plan was to become the blueprint for much of Sweden's later success under George Raynor. This is because a tactical system that placed reliance on basic passing skills and speed eliminated the necessity for highly skilled players. This formed the foundation of Bullock's success. At Bury, where financial resources were limited, it was simply not viable to rely on the directors continually purchasing high quality players to ensure success, which is why Bullock's system assumed greater value than the individual ability of each of the players. When Raynor worked in Sweden and the best players were being purchased by the big clubs in Europe, Raynor was forced to coach third and fourth string international players who, in spite of being less talented, succeeded due to teamwork and strategy. The success of such players in Olympic Games and World Cups was the remarkable legacy of Norman Bullock.

The man Bullock placed in the role of deep-lying centre forward was a young Geordie called Ernie Matthews. Matthews wasn't particularly big but did have a first-class shot on him and was a good passer of the ball. Bullock therefore worked on a plan to get the best out of both him and Bury's flying right-wingers by having Matthews play deeper than the conventional bustling 'English' centre forward.

He would receive balls from the half-backs and feed this directly to the wingers, and then either receive the pulled-back cross to convert once he arrived in the area himself, or allow an inside forward to steal into the space vacated by the absent centre-back and strike at goal.

Matthews would have to veer from the centre-forward position because he would get battered if he occupied the conventional spot in those rough Second Division matches of the 1930s. However, Matthews was essentially a deep-lying centre forward. Bullock thus applied Creek's philosophy: 'It is far better to take the players at your disposal, with their varied talents and abilities, and invent a scheme to suit them.'

The success of the player, allied to the intuitive way in which Bullock benefitted from Matthews, remained long in Raynor's mind and brought to him a realisation after the war that the *new reality* displayed by the Hungary team which beat England at Wembley was actually a reinvention of old tactics that had been quite commonplace in England before the war. 'There was nothing new about [a deep-lying centre forward],' wrote Raynor. 'It had often been used in British football before the war – but until Hidegkuti showed it at Wembley in 1953 it had been forgotten by most people at home, who thought it some new invention.'

Jonathan Wilson looks overseas and as far afield as Hungary in order to claim that the deep-lying centre forward was an idea that was first chanced upon by Marton Bukovi at MTK, in a post-war Hungary where the big strong centre forwards had all died in the war.

'If you didn't have the right style of centre forward' (Wilson reads into Bukovi's thinking) 'rather than trying to force unsuitable players into the position … it was better simply to do away with him altogether.'

Wilson, therefore, ignores what Bullock and others were doing years before Bukovi, although to be fair to Wilson, Norman Bullock wasn't exactly doing away with the centre forward, but discarding the battering ram and replacing it with the late arriving centre forward.

This method of the withdrawn forward would, of course, later be used by Raynor when he was in charge of Sweden, for it contained the germ of his 'G-man' concept. This was where one player would rove between the half-backs and the forwards to quickly convert defence into attack.

Bury had turned the corner, and a dramatic home win against Swansea in February 1936 helped them climb the table and to really start turning heads. That same month Arsenal manager George Allison, Derby manager George Jobey, and Clem Stephenson from Huddersfield, went along to Leicester City's Filbert Street to see Matthews and Chalmers score in a 2–1 away win for Bury. This was clear evidence that Bullock's system had elevated Bury's standing in the football world. Mr Robinson, Bury's chairman, warned all three of them of trying to buy any of Bury's players, and with Chalmers and Raynor playing alongside Matthews, a sound finish to the season was secured.

Raynor remembered his time at Bury positively. His emergence from discarded reserve to first-team regular at Gigg Lane seems to have given him the most pride of all when he looked back on his playing career. Indeed, Raynor's ethos was one of hard work and a determination to overcome: 'Throughout life you can find countless examples of people who have succeeded despite ... drawbacks and difficulties ... they have only succeeded, because they were willing to force themselves onwards to success no matter what happened.'

Things were looking up and a splendid start to the 1936/37 season planted a seed of great expectation in the minds of the Bury faithful. By the time the side played at Bradford City on 21 November 1936 they had only lost 2 of their first 16 matches. However, during the game, Raynor broke his left ankle in a tackle with Bradford's left-back Charlie McDermott. Inspired by support from league clubs and well wishers, Raynor soon pulled himself around, tossing away his crutches within two weeks of the injury and soldiering on using one stick, before undertaking exercises to hasten the mend of his broken leg.

Two consequences of this enforced lay-off can be presupposed, the first of which was that this was the beginning of the end for Raynor's footballing career. Thereafter he would suffer recurrent injuries throughout the rest of his playing career. The second consequence was that during his recuperation he would go along to Gigg Lane and see just what Norman Bullock was attempting to achieve tactically at the club. Raynor would mull over these ideas and put them to good use in his later career.

Raynor made his return at a match against Spurs in late March 1937 after being out of action for only four months, but by then Blackpool and Leicester had secured the promotion spots. Bury finished 3 points shy of promotion to the First Division. They were never again to get as close to the summit and neither would Raynor as a player, with a knee injury signalling the end of his time at Gigg Lane.

3

THE WAR
YEARS

In the summer of 1938, Bill McCracken offered Raynor a lifeline by asking him to join him at Aldershot to team up with his ex-Bury teammate Willie Chalmers in order to replicate their former successes. McCracken took full advantage of the fact that the two had formed such a promising partnership at Bury and now reasoned that he could bring Raynor down to Hampshire on the cheap, given the fact that he was injured and out of favour up North. Perhaps Chalmers had suggested or put the idea in McCracken's head. Raynor wrote later that 'McCracken came and said, "I will take you George. I will play you and risk the knee standing up. If it breaks down I will do something for you."' Raynor set up home with his wife at Haig Road.

Billy McCracken had been the right-back in the famous Newcastle United side of the early 1900s. McCracken was one of the players that crop up when discussion of the pre-1925 offside law is raised. Along with his defensive colleagues at St James' Park, he became adept at stifling the life out of opposing attacks by continually positioning himself to place forwards in offside positions. It could be said that McCracken was the diametric opposite of Norman Bullock. Bullock challenging convention, whereas McCracken remained allied to Chapman's 'WM' formation.

Indeed, even after the war he was still persisting with the WM when he was finally given the sack by the Aldershot board in 1949.

McCracken's reactionary mentality had been reflected in his managerial career; while it never achieved great heights, it was certainly far from plumbing the depths either, and drifted comfortably along in the median range of the Football League. He had cut his teeth at Hull City, managing the side when they had come oh-so-close to putting Arsenal out of the FA Cup in the semi-final of 1930. However, that same season Hull were relegated and McCracken went to try his luck instead with Gateshead. They missed out on promotion from the Third Division by a whisker, and then surprisingly (given the position he had got the club into) he upped sticks in the close season to go and manage Millwall. At Millwall, McCracken stagnated and despite a flash-in-the-pan victory when Gateshead were walloped in the cup in December 1936, the club stayed put in the Second Division, after which he left to take up the post at Aldershot vacated by Angus Seed. Seed had been at Aldershot for years, but the directors' hands had finally been forced when the side went 17 games without so much as a sniff of a win during the winter of 1936.

Under McCracken's guidance, Raynor was tutored in toeing the line and playing in the WM formation. Although that being said, McCracken's guidance in making George coach of the reserves and the advice he gave him upon becoming a coach would later prove invaluable.

During the 1938/39 season, Chalmers and Raynor teamed up particularly well with Cecil Ray, the centre forward, and between the three of them contributed 45 goals to the team's kitty. Nevertheless, Aldershot performed poorly that year going out to Runcorn in the FA Cup and suffering heavy defeats throughout the season. Raynor, McCracken and the rest of the club could hardly have imagined that the club was about to enter a halcyon period as the proverbial storm clouds gathered over Europe.

The 1939/40 season lasted 3 matches before the declaration of war, and Stanley Rous called on all footballers to offer their services to the nation. As a result of this a considerable number of professionals signed up to become Army Physical Training Instructors (APTIs), a good proportion of whom ended up being billeted at Aldershot where the training was organised. As the war effort was mobilised, some of the Football League's best players accepted the offer to become APTIs, and these included Joe Mercer, Cliff Britton, Tommy Lawton, Matt Busby, Stan Cullis, Don Welsh, Billy Cook, Arthur Cunliffe, Billy Wright, Archie Macauley, Norman Corbett, Bert Sproston and Eric Stephenson. Raynor, himself, signed up for service at the Reading recruitment office in November 1939 and became one of a number of APTIs who would later on apply the skills learnt during army training to their coaching careers.

As the league permitted players to guest for other sides during the war, it was McCracken's massive good fortune to be able to seek out the rich pickings – he would simply travel down to the barracks and see which APTIs were free to play on Saturday. Fancy a lower league club manager suddenly having his pick of some of the best British players in history? Well that's what fortune had come to Billy McCracken. McCracken would later say of team selection:

> I must say this about the officers down [in the barracks]. There were one or two good chiefs … When I went down to the camp I'd see the officer and he'd say 'morning, Mac' and I'd give him a big salute …
>
> 'Who do you want for Saturday?' he'd say.
>
> 'Well Sir,' I'd reply, 'it might be a bit difficult for you because the chara's leaving at so and so, you see.'
>
> 'You just tell me who're the players you want,' he'd say and he would work it for me.

Raynor's good fortune was in being able to play both against and on the same side as those players, which resulted in him befriending international players, a fact from which he would later reap rich dividends when seeking to win over the confidence of the Swedes in 1946.

As the stars started to arrive into Aldershot the club soon became a centre for representative fixtures, and Raynor was to star in a few of the charity matches held at the beginning of the war. He played for Aldershot against a combined Army Physical Training Corp (ATPC) and FA XI in October 1939 when Stanley Matthews and George Hardwick played for the combined XI, and the following month, now promoted to acting sergeant in the APTC, appeared for the Army XI that was beaten comprehensively by the FA XI at Reading. He recalled: 'I played for the then star-studded Aldershot side, along with such great players as Frank Swift [goalkeeper] and Tommy Lawton [centre forward]. I was on the right wing with Jimmy Hagan as my partner, and behind us was that prince of wing backs, Cliff Britton.' It took a little while for Aldershot to gel all the internationals together, but once Lawton was playing alongside Jimmy Hagan, it was instant fireworks. Lawton's penalty at Southampton in March 1940 was so strong it reportedly knocked the Saints' keeper into the back of the net with the ball. There is no doubt as to just how good those players were. Swift, Lawton, Hagan and Britton each appeared in the England wartime side. Joe Mercer, who also turned out for that England team, remarked about those players: 'This was a wonderful bunch to play with. I was lucky to be around at the same time. I have never played with [players] so eager to do well … everybody fancied himself a bit, everybody wanted the ball. Every time you gave a pass, you made nine enemies. The spirit was as keen as that.'

Playing alongside such players gave Raynor his first exposure to the big time as a player; he fitted in incredibly well with them and doesn't appear to have been overawed or outshone by the experience. Early in the 1941/42 season, during the London League fixture between Arsenal and Aldershot that was broadcast live on radio by the BBC, Raynor ran the legs off England international left-back Leslie Compton. This was the season during which Raynor made more appearances for the club than any of his illustrious teammates, and Aldershot finished fourth in the regionalised London League.

Raynor was good for his teammates too. Jimmy Hagan, the England inside right and wing partner to Raynor, represented England during the war, and after the 3–0 victory in the Auld Enemy tie in January 1942, the Aldershot programme proclaimed that Hagan had come to prominence as a result of his performances at Aldershot. 'There was some evidence that this was true,' writes Jack Rollin in *Soccer at War*, '[Hagan] played twice as many times in Aldershot's colours as he did for his own club Sheffield United [between 1939 and 1942].'

Raynor guested for Bournemouth at Aldershot's home fixture in November 1940 and would later appear as a guest for Clapton Orient, Charlton, Bury, Hull City and Crystal Palace. However, it was with Aldershot that he would enjoy his most productive and assured stay during the war years.

In the summer of 1940 the knee injury that had previously afflicted him and which would intermittently continue to cause him problems throughout the war years, became more severe. He was granted a military service exemption (MSE) from July 1940 until the October of that year: although he was able to play football throughout the 1940/41 'season' he was granted a further exemption from December 1943 until June 1944, while serving overseas.

Raynor was posted to North Africa towards the end of 1941 but this was not a permanent overseas posting because he played his last game for Aldershot in the 1942/43 season. Indeed, records received from the UK Ministry of Defence indicate that he was back in the UK in the summer of 1943.

In February 1943 he attended a course on physical training at Lamberhurst in Kent. The following month he was sent out to Baghdad and employed there by the Iraqi Ministry of Education to teach first at the Baghdad Physical Training Institute (PTI) and also at Dar Al-Mualameen School. According to Iraqi football historian, Hassanin Mubarak, Raynor's insistence that he was working for the Baghdad College in Iraq was wrong, he was actually working for the PTI (known locally as Mahad Al-Tarbiya Al-Badniya).

The director of the PTI at that time was another Englishman called Edward J. Sidebottom. Before taking up the post as director, Sidebottom had, reputedly, served as lecturer and director of youth activities and physical education at the Ministry of Education in Baghdad.

Raynor was then transferred to Basra, joining the Persia and Iraq Force (PAIF) to teach 'tough tactics and PT' to a bunch of raw army recruits. The idea was that these troops would be used as support for the 8th Army who were being mobilised to put down an Iraqi rebellion which, thankfully, never eventuated.

However, Raynor knocked his soldiers into line with incredible speed, and these troops eventually came to be used as occupation personnel in Basra instead. He quickly came to realise just what an opportunity had been presented to him in Iraq, a posting which protected him from the chaos and disruption of the war's front lines and demanded of him the marshalling and command of various training initiatives.

Raynor's innate ability to organise a plan of action seems to have first come to the fore during his active service. He rose very quickly to the rank of sergeant major, a status he never attempted to trade on, and after working in Basra got a job with the British Military Mission in Baghdad, where he was placed in charge of organising physical training and sport.

The troops on the ground in Iraq at the time were a mixture of sub-continentals and eastern Europeans, and Raynor would participate and referee in football matches between Greeks, Indians and local Iraqis. These games must have generated some interest because after hearing about the football being played at the Military Mission, the Prime Minister of Iraq sent word that he would like the Ministry of Education to organise an Iraqi team to tour the neighbouring Arab states. The initial request was handled by Sidebottom in Baghdad, who passed it on to Raynor in Basra and, hence, Raynor was recalled to the capital.

Rather than draw a representative side from all over Iraq, Raynor and Sidebottom decided to enlist the alumni at the Baghdad PTI to form the team that would go on tour and (for the first time) represent Iraqi football against the neighbouring Arab states.

The Institute was populated by army officers and university students, so was a reliable source of competent, fit and disciplined players who would be quicker and easier to knock into shape; in view of the difficulties Raynor would experience later when asked to form a gymnastic team from locals, it was a sound decision.

Raynor organised trial matches and from those games was able to reduce the number of aspirants to a manageable twenty players who he wished to take on tour. Ismail Mohammed, one graduate from the Institute, was a member of Raynor's team and went on to coach the Iraqi national team in 1957. The players were keen, obviously, to represent an Iraqi national team for the first time and all manner of ructions and fights broke out between candidates before the final twenty were selected. That was not the worst of it however, for there would also be some hairy moments during the course of what was meant to be a friendship tour.

The tour took place in March 1943. It would comprise 5 matches. The details of the tour were as follows (with thanks and acknowledgment to Hussanin Mubarak for these details):

01/03/1944 Beirut   'Iraq' 1–4 Lebanon
05/03/1944 Beirut   'Iraq' 1–2 American University of Beirut
08/03/1944 Damascus 'Iraq' 1–2 La Sagesse
10/03/1944 Damascus 'Iraq' 4–3 Syria
12/03/1944 Damascus 'Iraq' A–A Syria

The tour ended in Damascus at the racecourse. Raynor had been told by the commissioner of police in Damascus to expect some trouble from the thousand or so excitable spectators, but what actually happened was that the French Police and the Damascus Security Force – hardly the best of friends – started exchanging insults during the game, and then someone decided to fire a gun. A fire fight ensued. Eight people died and 200 were injured. In later years, while giving a speech, Raynor wryly remarked: 'That was my introduction to big time football!'

Otherwise the tour (although hardly a tremendous success on the field) did much to raise the profile of the British contingent in the Gulf States at that strangely innocent time. George was to comment: 'The success did British prestige the world of good, and whatever may be the case today, in those days the British were highly thought of in Iraq.'

Along with Sidebottom, Raynor was also asked to create a gymnastic team which was to give a display for the Iraqi royals. To assist in this, Raynor had an assault course built at the Physical Training School which he used to test the local Iraqis and that served, ultimately, only to confirm to him that the locals were idlers who were quite happy to bunk off out of sight at the first opportunity and go for a rest. This was put into sharp relief when he observed a heavily pregnant woman who would be forced to walk miles to market, a baby strapped to her side, to sell fruit for the sake of her children and herself.

Initially Raynor, overcome with sympathy for those who were apparently injured while tackling the assault course, organised for ambulances to be readily available. But he soon wised up to the ruse that the locals were employing – feigning injury and then taking a break under the welcome shade of the ambulances – and removed the ambulances from sight. Comparing the relative merits of Iraqi, Indian and British soldiers, he concluded that what separated the first two from the third was a 'heart to drive the body forward,' and that willpower and determination were the key determinants of success; therefore encouraging those qualities in others was the key to success not only in life, but also in sport. 'It was this belief that made me determined to become a coach when I left the Army,' he wrote. In the end the gymnastic display was a success, with the dignitaries and grandees of Baghdad society no doubt amazed by Raynor's ability to get such an impressive response out of the slackers and idlers he had been put in charge of.

Raynor was later also teaching at Dar Al-Mualameen according to a player called Hassan 'Fury' Karim. Raynor was employed there by the Ministry of Education; however, after agreeing a wage, there was some kind of problem with the rent of his lodgings and he left the country.

Raynor returned to England in the summer of 1945 with two glowing recommendations in his hand. One was from the Chief of General Staff in May 1945 ('His devotion to duty was a high inspiration – beyond praise – to all who served under him') and the other came from Nuri Pasha al-Said, the anglophile Prime Minister of Iraq at the time, whose reference for Raynor found its way into the inbox of Stanley Rous, the secretary of the Football Association.

Brian Glanville has, perhaps harshly, written that Rous had a high opinion only of those he shared seating with in the Royal Box at Wembley. If that was the case, however, then the reference from the Iraqi hierarchy for the Hoyland miner's son would not have done Raynor any harm whatsoever.

Just as Raynor's coaching career was developing, so changes were taking place in England.

In 1946, Rous was to finally succeed in getting Walter Winterbottom (a bookish graduate from the Carnegie College of Physical Education in Leeds) employed in the roles of both England national team manager and, primarily, Director of Coaching at the Football Association. The appointment concurred with Rous' view that coaching should form the basis of the post-war development of English football. Rous didn't stop there and in the years immediately following the war actively sought to encourage new ideas into the game. In the late 1940s the *FA Yearbook* was first published by Naldrett, as was the *FA Book for Boys*.

Ever the academic, Winterbottom oversaw the development of these publications, and it shows. They bucked a publishing trend in which results took precedence over performance. Both publications soon began to feature articles from foreign coaches and associations, and the England match reports were purposefully written in a dispassionate and even tone, with no blind adherence to the faith in the three lions, but a balanced view as to how the match was played out. In the *FA Book for Boys*, Winterbottom was given ample opportunity to state his piece on coaching and the benefits of training. George Raynor himself was asked to provide an article on boys' football in Sweden in the 1950s.

Now in possession of a letter of introduction and two shining references for George Raynor, Rous wrote back, promising him help in getting work once he got back to England. Rous' intention was no doubt genuine, but unfortunately the opportunities for actually finding Raynor the type of work that he obviously could excel at were almost non-existent in British football.

Much as Rous would have liked to have imposed an agreement on the Football League clubs to embrace coaching, the clubs themselves simply did not share his view. This reluctance to consider new ideas and methods to coincide with the advent of the new post-war world was not confined to the professional clubs either.

Rous, Winterbottom and now Raynor all appeared to be fighting an uphill battle to persuade English football sides to 'believe' in coaching. This opposition to coaching has been well-recorded by Bob Ferrier in his book *Soccer Partnership*. The resistance, wrote Ferrier, was from 'every quarter' and took 'many forms. There was resistance to the very idea of having an England team manager; there was resistance to pre-match training sessions and meetings of players; there was resistance to the whole, new, ambitious Football Association plan for a national coaching programme.'

Raynor returned to Britain in time for the 1945/46 season, when McCracken selected him for one game against Brighton, after which he was approached by the Aldershot Board to take on a trainer's role for the team. He started training the reserve side in November of 1945 at £5 per week. Raynor hardly shone from the off in his new role. The reserves were playing in the Third Division South Cup (South) qualifying competition that season and finished second bottom in an eleven-team league with 3 wins from 16 matches.

McCracken now gave Raynor some timeless advice: 'Don't pretend you know it all, or you will get no help. You are a nice humble fellow and if you keep that way everyone will confide in you.'

Such was his enthusiasm to train and coach, that in his spare time Raynor would also make other enquiries of clubs, only to discover just how few opportunities existed, but the degree of closed-mindedness which met any of his suggestions; indeed this blinkered attitude extended to all aspects of English football, particularly at the very top. With an eye on the future, Raynor considered that the time was now if Britain wanted to maintain the standards that the English national team had displayed during the war. 'British football needed a flow of properly coached and instructed youngsters to come into the league sides and make sure that the British countries remained on top of the football world.'

It is interesting that Raynor should have a vision not only for the English national side, but for the game generally in England. It was clearly an idea, however, that otherwise went unheeded. It's reasonable to conclude that Raynor's international experiences, when he had been given overall control to plan and deliver successful initiatives, put him very much out of kilter with football people in Britain, to whom systemic change was a risk to their localised control.

Football had served these people well before and during the war, and would certainly continue to do so for many years afterwards. As a result clubs could see no reason to embrace radical ideas intended to ultimately help the English national side when the clubs were enjoying the benefits of mass popularity with neither the need nor any call for change. Stan Mortensen described the mood aptly when he later told David Miller: '… Tactics weren't a part of the game [in those days] … We were still playing totally attacking football. That was what the crowds at home expected … People wanted attacking football, and that's what they got.'

At this point, on hearing that the Prime Minister in Iraq wished to hold a youth tournament in Iraq, Rous earmarked Raynor to organise it; something that due to his reserve

coaching at Aldershot, he was unable to do. However, at the end
of 1945/46 McCracken told Raynor that there was no future
for him at Aldershot. This was probably no more than an issue
of cost-saving in the immediate post-war years, as at no point
either then or in the future did Raynor ever have an axe to
grind against McCracken or Aldershot.

When Aldershot let Raynor go in 1946, Rous had encouraged
him to see if he could get work with the Hampshire Football
Association. It proved to be a dead end: Raynor declared,
'Wherever I went I found people believing that it would take
at least two years for football to get under way again, and until
that time coaching was quite out of the question.' Stanley Rous
persevered, and one day put pen to paper to tell George of a
coaching position brought to his attention by the Swedish
Football Association. Had it not been for that letter, Raynor
might well have drifted out of football forever.

4

OPPORTUNITES
IN SWEDEN

Britain's reluctance toward coaching was a view not shared on the European mainland. The Swedes had embraced coaching footballers and the impact had been felt at the very grassroots of the game there. In the schools of Sweden the schoolboys received a standard of coaching that was better than that provided to English professional players at that time. Indeed, the standard of coaching in Swedish schools in the 1940s and 1950s has never been equalled in Britain because, even when a programme encouraging football coaching was introduced by the Football Association and the Board of Education in the late 1930s, it was made neither compulsory nor was it extended to actually coaching the teachers. However, in the 1940s, Sweden had teachers who were taught how to coach football.

In terms of their national team, a strategic change had also come about. Before the war, the Swedish attitude to a national football coach had been in keeping with their view of football generally: short-term and amateur. During the war the Swedish National Association decided to dispense with one person to select, coach and manage the national team and instead to use a selection committee, the Uttagningskommitténor (the UK). This committee was responsible for selecting the squad for each match, with the chairman, 'Putte' Kock, who had won a Bronze at the 1924 Paris Olympics, taking over coaching duties.

Kock's importance to the development of the game in Sweden in those post-war years cannot be over-emphasised, primarily because of his friendship and support of Raynor. His appointment as national coach was initially only intended to be a stopgap during the war; when it ended, his tactical limitations were exposed when Sweden lost comprehensively to Switzerland in 1945. As a direct result of that game, the Swedish National Association contacted the Football Association to enquire as to whether they could recommend a British coach to prepare and train the national team.

The British football fraternity were held in high regard in Scandinavia. Stanley Rous, in his book *Football Worlds*, wrote:

> In 1946, as these [Scandinavian] countries tried to re-establish the game after their bleak football-less years, they turned to the Football Association for assistance in coaching. We readily agreed and some fifteen coaches went to Norway and Sweden in the close season. So successful was this experiment that the Swedish FA asked us to find them a national coach. The man I proposed was something of a surprise to them, since George Raynor was an almost unknown Third Division footballer.

Why Rous should volunteer George Raynor for Sweden when others were perhaps more qualified for such a role, is a question the answer to which can only be guessed at. The greatest likelihood is that the Iraqi Prime Minister's reference was still fresh in Rous' mind when the communication from the Swedes was received into his offices. Similarly, by making this recommendation Rous was making good his promise to get Raynor fixed up in a coaching role.

Whereas the decision was convenient for Rous, it was hardly ideal for Raynor, back from a long stint in the Middle East and suddenly being recommended to leave Britain once again when his heart had been set on coaching football in Britain. He was later to write: 'I didn't want to go abroad. I had spent long enough abroad in the Army and I now wanted to work for the game in Britain. I told Sir Stanley so.' What ultimately convinced him to accept the appointment in Sweden was probably due to a combination of Rous' authority and the lack of reception at home to his ideas of coaching. There may also have been a far more basic financial reason: the needs arising from having a young family.

George Raynor arrived in Sweden, stepping from a steamship onto a gangway at Gothenburg docks in March 1946. The only person there to greet him was Putte Kock. Kock was evidently underwhelmed by the tiny Yorkshireman: 'What a little man! And so silent.'

Both men were, for their own reasons, quite nervous about the appointment. Until a few months beforehand, Raynor had been coach to the reserves at Aldershot and yet here he was, the prospective coach to a national team! For Kock, Raynor's appointment was hardly a God-send; rather than providing a manager from one of the league's famous clubs, Stanley Rous had instead sent an utter unknown, a coach from an army town in Hampshire. The Swedish press would be unforgiving if the gamble to bring in a foreign coach for the first time fell flat, and Kock understood very well the risks he was taking as chairman of the national selection committee.

Perhaps this shared apprehension helped in cementing what would become a life-long friendship between Raynor and Kock, a friendship that would serve Swedish football well. With Kock's friendship, Raynor would go on to introduce ideas, secure in the knowledge that he would have unstinting support at national level with regard to his team-building, tactics and preparation.

Much later, Raynor admitted that their relationship did not always go swimmingly, but overall he and Kock shared a mutual respect. When asked about the two, John Eriksson (the centre forward who played for Sweden in the famous 2–2 draw with Hungary in 1953) stated that Kock and Raynor had 'much the same mentality'. Eriksson remembered Kock teaching Raynor to sing Swedish songs while accompanying him on the piano, and George would later write affectionately that '[Putte] was a great leader, jovial and shrewd and he loved the headlines ... [He] was a great mixer and well respected by all clubs and players. He knew them all and all respected him.' In return, Kock would devote an entire chapter to the Yorkshireman in his 1955 book *Fotbollen – Mitt Ode*.

The Swedish print media were not, however, interested in any tales of a fluffy friendship between the two. In Stockholm concerns were expressed in the national newspapers as to whether Raynor could be trusted with such an important job. It says much about his talent away from the football field that he was very quickly able to get the press onside with shrewd manipulation.

When Raynor arrived in Gothenburg the international selection committee – the people he had to report to – consisted of Kock, Joel Bjorkman (a former player with GAIS in Gothenburg), Thure Claesson (a former player with Falkenburg) and the secretary, Axel Bergqvist, a former referee and secretary of the national Referee's Committee. The committee was to remain staffed with the same personnel until 1949 when Eric Persson (chairman of Malmo) replaced Bergqvist and later, when Kock was sacked in 1956, Persson would take over Kock's role as chairman. The committee provided stability in terms of personnel and ideas; it also provided a platform which enabled those ideas to be rolled out and accepted by the clubs. This was because it was comprised of respected and well-connected individuals from the leading and most powerful clubs, and as a result the clubs were not resistant to ideas once set down by the national committee if those plans could be seen to benefit the national side.

Raynor had been employed to provide Sweden with a strong national side. To do this he needed to cultivate the confidence of the clubs and have the freedom to work with them. To varying degrees, each of the clubs allowed him access to players and welcomed his presence during club training sessions; they also welcomed his input, even to the extent of him suggesting positional changes for specific players. Bengt Agren, a member of the 1958 World Cup Organising Committee, commented: 'In the first two years of his contract, George Raynor helped to prepare the national team before internationals but he was also there to help the coaches in the clubs of the First Division to bring to them a new way of thinking.' The case of Bertil Nordahl, the Degerfors full-back, is a good example of this. Raynor wrote:

> I realised that [Bertil] was the man for the centre-half job, but ... was told that ... his true role was that of a full-back. But I wanted him at centre-half back because he was a player with some bite ... The only way I could secure Nordahl as a centre-half was to go and see his club [Degerfors IF] and to coach him that way. I spent several spells with him and it was this close contact with the clubs that brought us our success.

Raynor had noted that Nordahl was strong and tough, but his natural attacking inclination meant that he would blindly charge off up-field leaving a big gap in his centre-half position, which the opposition would exploit. Raynor succeeded in correcting this fault by coaching Nordahl to maintain a defensive mentality while the player was still at Degerfors. It says much about the Swedish culture and their apparent desire to succeed at that time that the clubs adopted such an accommodating attitude and were happy to allow the national coach to interfere with club tactics.

In Sweden there was a definite inclination on the part of the clubs, coaches and players to help the National Association achieve its principle aim in securing success for the national side. Such an initiative could only have happened with the blessing of the coaches, including Lajos Czeizler, the vastly travelled Hungarian coach of Norkopping, the club of Gunnar Nordahl and the most successful of the Swedish clubs at that time. To assume that Sweden's success arose as a result of Raynor and Kock alone would be to do all of the league clubs and their personnel a huge disservice. Coming himself from a community unified by a common purpose, one can see how the benefits of a strategy of national unity would have come as second nature to Raynor.

Raynor saw his job primarily as being an advisor, writing: 'I advised the selectors about the types of players I wanted.' This was an important factor to begin with, as the selectors knew the players who were available. It was only after 1949, when Raynor had immersed himself in and really knew the game in Sweden, that he got to vote as to who should be selected for the national side. When Raynor returned to Sweden in 1956 to prepare the side for the 1958 World Cup, however, it was as an adviser with no vote on selection. 'This,' he wrote, 'was by far the better arrangement, for in effect I gave the selectors advice which they always took, but the responsibility of selection was solely theirs.' There was a strange aspect to the arrangement. If Raynor advised on having a certain player in the team then, as we shall see, the selection committee would rubber stamp that approval; however, the arrangement took the pressure off him completely, freeing him to concentrate on coaching the players and was an important contributory factor to the success that Raynor had during that tournament.

Raynor identified key challenges when he first watched football in Sweden: one of the first was the rarity of tough tackling players. The Swedes did not have the full-blooded challenges that were such a feature of the English professional game from where Raynor had come. In Sweden, Raynor found lots of players who were content to pass the ball short, and many others who were good at keeping possession, but he noted that there were very few players who wanted to 'get stuck in'. The reliance on possession made the Swedish game laboured and predictable and that lack of bite invited problems when the team lost possession. To Raynor's mind, Swedish football was 'without punch' and the scarcity of players willing to go on the field to compete had been ignored in favour of what Raynor saw as the typical 'continental approach' with its 'pretty close-passing game'.

Raynor decided that to achieve success Sweden would have to adopt a much more effective way of playing, and that what he needed to do was to unite English and Swedish football. The emphasis would be on playing the game far faster than the Swedes had been accustomed to. Raynor would encourage the development in the clubs of tough-tackling midfielders so that the team could counter-attack opponents quickly and effectively. It was with this tactic that Bullock had succeeded at Bury. Raynor wanted to replicate the same ideas with Sweden.

Raynor was not averse to mixing and matching Continental and British 'elements' because, as he accepted, the long ball pass to open up a defence could be just as effective as the short pass but he wanted to 'create' a new type of Swedish footballer: the type of players who could combine the skills and technique of the Swedish player with the tough-tackling mentality of the typical league player in England. These factors would later manifest themselves during the 1958 World Cup. The ascent of players like Sigge Parling, nicknamed 'the iron stove', was a good example of the strong, destructive player Raynor wanted. In the semi-final of that World Cup, Parling would escape punishment after a full-blooded challenge on Fritz Walter which left the Germans with ten fit men and the game still on a knife-edge. In the final itself, Sweden's first goal, skilfully scored by Nils Liedholm, came via an arrow-like 40–yard pass from the right-half position which Agne Simonsson did well to control on the right-wing, before playing it inside to Liedholm.

These were the tough, hardy crops which Raynor had sowed.

Another factor Raynor identified was a cultural one. Football in Sweden was an amateur game. If a footballer became a professional, that player could not be considered for further selection to the national side, and the effects of this policy would be keenly felt after the 1948 Olympic victory, when Sweden were arguably the best side in Europe. Following their Olympic victory, Sweden's best players would be signed by Italian, French and Spanish clubs, and taking the national side onwards while labouring under this immense handicap was to be an almighty challenge within itself. There is no question that Sweden's failure to qualify for the 1954 World Cup had much to do with the fact that they had lost all their best players to professional clubs throughout Europe.

Added to this was the fact that amateur footballers have to be employed by someone, somewhere. Gathering players together for the national squad was a minor miracle in itself which owed much to the good grace of the many employers who lost workers every time a training camp was organised. Holger Bergerus, later the secretary of the Swedish Football Association, wrote in the *FA Yearbook* in 1952 of the realities that confronted the National Association: 'Each year the Swedish Selection Committee arranges a training-camp for the International team. It would be ideal to have more courses for International players, but this cannot be realised as Swedish players are amateurs and thus find it difficult to get away.'

5

OLYMPIC
GOLD

Raynor's baptism into Swedish national life was at first courted by doubt and suspicion; other than having the blessing of Stanley Rous, the Swedish had no idea who the little Yorkshireman was. The Stockholm press were suspicious that they had been sent 'a nobody', particularly when at a reception following a game between Birmingham City and Stockholm on 17 May 1946, the touring players told the Stockholm reporters that they had no idea who George Raynor was.

However, shortly after the Birmingham team left, Raynor experienced a stroke of luck. An RAF side containing international players Stanley Matthews and George Hardwick, the England captain, arrived on tour from Norway. Both players had been on duty for the English national side which had just played the Swiss, and Matthews was an international star, renowned throughout Europe.

Raynor met the RAF players at a reception held in their honour, renewing his acquaintance with them from the representative matches which he had featured in when playing for Aldershot during the war. When the Swedes noticed the familiarity between Raynor and the famous Stanley Matthews, it did much to dispel their doubts; but the meeting proved to be an even greater blessing for Raynor, desperate for any information he might be able to get about the Swiss side which Sweden were due to play for his second game in charge of the national side on 7 July 1946.

It should be noted that Raynor's first match as Swedish coach was actually a game played against Denmark. This resulted in a 3–1 defeat for Sweden and added to the general mood that the Swedish FA had made something of a mistake in accepting Rous' suggestion that Raynor was the coach for them. However, early mistakes were to be expected and having viewed the players at his disposal, Raynor reportedly said to Bergerus that 'with the players you have in this country you won't lose to [Denmark] again in the next ten years'.

England's game with Switzerland at Stamford Bridge on 11 May 1946 had given them plenty to think about. After an hour's play it seemed that the Swiss might even become the first foreign side to beat England on their own soil, with the home side's attacks coming to nothing and Friedlaender scoring to put the Swiss one up. Raich Carter finally got the equaliser in the 66th minute, running onto a wall pass from Tommy Lawton. This cracked the Swiss lock and by the 78th minute Brown, Lawton and Carter had put England 4–1 ahead, but the margin of victory was hardly reflective of the game.

The Times of 13 May 1946 reported:

> It was easy to see why Switzerland have made such a name for themselves. Tactically they play the old-fashioned style of football. The centre half back comes up into attack and with the wing halves, who play wide, they have in effect eight forwards who sweep the ball from one to another at speed and on the ground ... In attack England played with an easy nonchalance ... Brown and Carter without the close attention of the wing half backs, had a field day in the open spaces, but for all their dribbling and prompting England lacked that vital thrust in front of goal ... when half-time came with no score Switzerland had done enough for one to realize that if England were to win, they would have to stop playing exhibition football and give up keeping the ball too close.

What was quite clear was that the Swiss encouraged short passing from the opposition. If the inside forwards had the ball and were not challenged they would invariably cut inside to make a short pass into a heavily manned defence. In this game, the Swiss left-back Willi Steffen (Lawton's Chelsea teammate and, reportedly, the best left-back in the world at the time) did a fantastic man-marking job on Lawton, and England's conventional attacks petered out in the face of a congested Swiss defence.

Raynor quizzed Matthews and Hardwick about the way Switzerland had played. Both were able to provide insight but Matthews in particular proved a vital source of information, because as a forward player he had first-hand knowledge of how the Swiss organised their defence. 'Matthews and Hardwick explained how the Swiss left-back played in the middle, taking on the role of our centre-half back, leaving the wing half backs to cover the opposing wingers and the centre-half back to act as an attacker.'

Tactically speaking this was the 'Bolt' defensive system devised by the Swiss coach Karl Rappan, and using this system of defence, Switzerland had been relatively successful. They had beaten England and Germany in the 1930s and in November 1945 had easily beaten Sweden 3–0 in Geneva; now, using the same tactic against England in 1946, they had once again caused problems. The Bolt system relied on the full-backs playing centrally behind one another.

As Raynor noted, it was a very prescriptive manner of play.

A conventional WM attack like England's had difficulty overcoming this system. Whereas Matthews could beat his wing-back when he did cross the ball, he would find the Swiss centre half would be marking the English inside forward, and the centre forward would be marked by the left-back. What's more, if the English committed themselves to attack, it would leave space for the Swiss centre half, inside forwards and forwards to create a six-man attack.

George Raynor reasoned that because Rappan ascribed specific roles to his players, the key to confounding the Swiss defence would be to confront them with an unconventional attack. Raynor decided that the best way of overcoming this was to instruct his centre forward, Gunnar Nordahl, and his right-wing pairing of Gunnar Gren and Olly Nyberg to play well up the field of play to exploit the defensive weakness on the left of the Swiss defence. Meanwhile, on the left-wing, Nystrom would play conventionally and, if he could beat his marker, would leave the Swiss a man light down that flank. To link the centre halves and the attacking line, Raynor would use Bertil Nordahl as his G-man. By playing in this way Raynor would pull the defence out of shape, push them back and, if Sweden were to lose possession, the Swedes were to attack the ball aggressively.

The 'G-man' was Raynor's euphemism for a player (normally centrally placed) who would orchestrate attacks and was a throw-back to the days of Ernie Matthews at Bury in the mid-1930s.

He placed Bertil Nordahl (the brother of Gunnar and Knut) into this role, letting him go wherever he wanted, attracting either the centre half or the inside forwards as he went. Behind Bertil he played Rune Emanuelsson, who he described as 'a good getter of the ball' with the instruction that he was to win the ball and play it to Bertil. John 'Jompa' Eriksson, who later played alongside Emanuelsson for the national side, described his colleague in the following way: 'Rune wasn't a technically gifted footballer but he was strong and he had a big heart too and he used to really fight for the ball with the opponents.'

It says much about Raynor that, fresh out of the reserve ranks at Aldershot, here he was immediately facing a challenge set by one of Europe's foremost football academics and cleverly discarding convention to meet that challenge. Armed with the belief that there was a weakness in Rappan's system, Raynor invited the press into the training session to let them see how the players were able to discuss tactics; this was in fact a smokescreen as the plan he had in mind for the Swiss had already been formed.

Allowing the players to discuss matters freely gave them the belief – correctly – that their views were valuable and of consequence. This was excellent man-management on the part of Raynor, and was warmly received by the players who not only had a real hunger to learn about the game, but welcomed the opportunity to participate in team talks. Just as importantly, these team talks allowed him to make sure that the players understood their roles implicitly. If the result went as Raynor thought it would, he would have the admiration of the unsupportive, still suspicious press and the respect of the players. It was a calculated gamble on his part.

Switzerland scored first, but Gren and then Nystrom on the left-wing put Sweden 2 up before the break. After the interval though, there was a veritable avalanche of Swedish goals – 5 altogether, with Gren scoring 3 more: a conclusive 7–2 thrashing of Karl Rappan's famously defensive Switzerland.

No team, not even the Hungarians, were ever to inflict such a defeat on the Swiss: 'That victory made me,' wrote Raynor. 'And Stanley Rous visiting Stockholm shortly afterwards, told the Swedes that I was one of the best coaches in the world and would put their football right on top.' Once Raynor had satisfied the circumspect public, his attention and that of the National Association turned toward preparing for what would be the real test of the national side, the 1948 Olympic Games, which in March 1946 had been awarded to London.

Under Raynor's guidance the Swedish National XI was soon proving to be capable of much that was good in football; scoring 30 goals in 6 internationals, Europe was suddenly sitting up and taking notice of the side.

Later that year Norkopping arrived in England during the Swedish close season. Five times winners of the Swedish League during the war years and twice Swedish Cup winners, they flew into Northolt on 28 October 1946 and embarked on a short, unbeaten tour of England. Presided over by Carl Eric Hallden and managed by Czeizler, the squad included Nils Liedholm, Gunnar and Knut Nordahl. The English teams were some of the top professional sides of the day. Wolves had just missed out on winning the First Division title by a single point from Liverpool, and a few months before the tour, Charlton had won the FA Cup at Wembley. It must have been something of an embarrassment to the professionals of Charlton, Newcastle, Wolves and Sheffield United (who they beat out of sight at Brammall Lane 5–2), not to have been able to beat a bunch of mechanics, firemen and pastry chefs from Sweden.

International recognition followed for the Swedes: in May 1947 Gunnar Nordahl and Gren were selected for the Rest of Europe side against Great Britain at Hampden Park to celebrate Britain's return to FIFA. Nordahl (typically tank-like) equalised in the first half with a snap shot on the turn inside the goal area.

Given his sudden elevation, one can appreciate how much it would have meant to Raynor when an international match between Sweden and England was organised to be played in November 1947 at Highbury Stadium. This was an attempt on the part of the Swedish FA to really test what they now felt were the makings of the Olympic side against top international opposition. The success of the Swedish side had not gone unnoticed across the North Sea; before the impending international, Geoffrey Green wrote intelligently in *The Times* of the threat posed at that time by Sweden to England's unbeaten home record, baldly stating that 'the prestige of our game in these islands will be at stake'.

England were coming to the end of the most wondrous period in their national side's history: the 8–0 victory over Scotland in 1943, the 10–0 victory in Lisbon in 1947 and the astonishing 4–0 victory against Italy in Turin (played in 1948, the year before Italy lost those great Torino players at Superga) are easily the most impressive victories in England's international football history. During the war, England's side was magnificent: Frank Swift, George Hardwick, Laurie Scott, Joe Mercer, Stan Cullis, Cliff Britton, Stanley Matthews, Jimmy Hagan, Tommy Lawton, Raich Carter and Tom Finney. They were players capable of beating the best teams in the world and made the wartime England XI one of the greatest international teams in history. Now, in 1947, with just one or two changes to that side, they would face Sweden.

So much in awe of his peers was Raynor that at the end of the game at Highbury he bagged a schoolboy's autograph sheet of the entire English side for his nephew.

Years later he commented: 'A Swedish victory at Highbury would have been unthinkable, because England had a very strong side at that time, but the result was of secondary importance. What mattered was that my players should have the experience of meeting such a strong team, and their performance would give me valuable clues as to the weakness and strength of my own side.'

Raynor once again changed the system he would use: against England he would keep close to Norman Bullock's principles, but now by switching the roving role and playing Gunnar Nordahl at centre forward as the G-man. Stan Mortensen wrote later: 'What a match they gave us! They played in a style … strange to us, with Gunnar Nordahl refusing to go up with our centre-half, but rather hanging back away from him to pick up the loose ball and help the other forwards.'

Sweden would lose the match which, probably, explains why the significance of Gunnar Nordahl playing as a withdrawn centre forward did not have the same impact that Hidegkuti's play would have on British football thinking following 1953 when Don Revie and Ronnie Allen would ape his positioning. However, there was very little difference in the way in which Gunnar Nordahl (at Highbury in 1947) and Hidegkuti (at Wembley in 1953) played.

By half-time England had a 2-goal lead, but halfway through the first half Nordahl had grabbed a goal from a free-kick. As Geoffrey Green was to write, with the score at 3–1 'England had nothing to worry about. That perhaps was the trouble.'

Raynor used the half-time team talk to reinforce the values he was seeking to impose into the Swedish game: 'We hadn't been strong enough in the tackle, we hadn't been getting the ball … I told my men to get into the tackle quicker, to mark better and keep the ball away from England. They responded magnificently and completely dominated the second half.'

Billy Wright, the England wing half, noted that the second-half performance of the Swedish side was astonishing: 'Time and again they had us on the run and seemed to have terrific reserves of strength.'

According to Wright, it was an open secret that the Swedish team took 'pep pills' during the interval. He quoted Raynor as saying, 'Our men certainly showed their best form after taking them, but I am not prepared to say whether the pills which have a sugar basis had a physical or only a psychological effect. Whatever it was, the Swedish players gave of their best in the second half.'

Right after the kick-off, Swift in the England goal was beaten by a shot but Hardwick, covering, headed off the line. With the Swedish wing half-backs attacking and the English losing control of the midfield, Sweden 'became a very real menace'. With 20 minutes to go, Gren scored from the penalty spot to bring the score to 2–3. 'Here we were,' wrote Stan Mortensen, 'fighting to save a game against a team playing inspired football. They had quite a crowd of supporters with them, and they packed together and shouted in unison under the direction of a cheerleader, Yankee baseball fashion. With 10 minutes to go, they attacked so heavily that it seemed certain they would make a draw or even inflict on England their first-ever defeat at home by a Continental side.' It was a close-run thing as the game neared its final stages. This was a game, remember, when England were playing against genuinely amateur players.

Just before the end, Mortensen scored the clincher; a goal that Tom Finney later ranked as the finest he had ever seen. Mortensen, with typical modesty, later described the goal in his autobiography: '... the Swedish keeper (Lindberg) took a goal-kick, and did not get hold of it properly. I was standing about forty yards from goal, and instead of the ball clearing me, it only carried to me. I was able to kill it and to get into my stride at once. I forged ahead for goal ... and everything came off for me. The ball ran kindly, I held off a tackle or two, and I was able to keep my balance for the final shot.'

It was a very close game and, as Green wrote, 'England had been made to think'. It was also a result that was to leave a lasting impression in England and Europe. Two years later Green remembered that England had been run 'to the last yard' and writing in 1960, Bernard Joy wrote that the performance was the springboard for Sweden, proving to them 'that nothing could shake their resolve to carry off the Olympic title in London a year later'.

Perhaps England's victory mitigated the impact of the Swedish performance in the public mind. The result meant that the opportunity to learn lessons from the victory was lost. However, lessons learned that day were not lost in Europe.

Sweden's performance and tactics would have been analysed and discussed throughout Europe; England and English football was big news then and any team losing in such a close match would have been the focus of debate overseas. It is most likely that the game would have been read about in Hungary where news regarding the deep-lying role occupied by Gunnar Nordahl would have been received with interest.

Raynor now had the makings of a strong, attack-minded Olympic team but he needed to consolidate the side with a tough-tackling midfielder; consequently he advised the committee to bring the wing-back Birger Rosengren back into the team. Rosengren had played only 1 game for the national side in 1945. The selection committee convened two training camps in March and May of 1948. After the second of these the side played Holland (coached at the time by Jesse Carver) in Amsterdam, losing 1–0, and then in July did excellently to beat the Austrians 3–2 in Solna.

Raynor wrote that he was less worried about the results than about the lack of penetration from the wings; he also had concerns about some defensive issues. In August, just before the team left for London, they convened again at Hindas, near Gothenburg, during which they were organised to play what they were led to believe was a light-hearted trial match where players were deliberately played out of position.

It was in this game that Raynor moved Kjell Rosen, a left-wing half to the outside-right position. This move had been inspired by Kjell's own performances against Austria and Holland where he had tended to attack down the flank without care for the position he had vacated.

The wing-half positions were made up of Rosengren 'the destroyer', Bertil Nordahl in the centre-half position, with the disciplined defensive approach instilled by Raynor's coaching supplementing his attacking zeal, and at left-wing half, Sune Andersson, an attacking midfielder.

Now that Raynor had moved Rosen up front he could afford to have Andersson add to the attack from the left-half position without exposing the defence unnecessarily. This worked especially well with the left-wing pairing of Carlsson and Liedholm during the competition. Henry Carlsson's play at inside left was so impressive that Raynor was now forced to move Nils Liedholm to the outside-left position. Throughout his coaching career Raynor was quite willing to rely on his wingers to give shape to his attack. This appears to be last minute tinkering but, as Raynor noted, such was the ability of Liedholm to play anywhere that the decision to move him to the wing proved to be inspired.

6

OLYMPIC
GLORY

There were a few oddities regarding the 1948 Olympic football tournament, one of which was the fact that although it was an international tournament there were British coaches leading many of the teams. Indeed it could be said that ironically (at a time when Britain was so reluctant to accept coaching) the tournament represented the high water mark for British-born coaches. In addition to George Raynor, Reg Mountford coached Denmark, Eric Keen the Egyptians, and Jesse Carver (who Raynor would meet later in his career) Holland.

Meanwhile, Matt Busby, the Manchester United manager, had accepted an invitation from the Football Association to coach the Great Britain team. Busby, however, later wrote that winning the league title with Manchester United 'was child's play' compared to organising the Britain's Olympic team. Although he brought a real sense of professionalism to the position (he insisted on being joined by Tom Curry, United's trainer and Ted Dalton, the United physiotherapist), Busby would find himself bewildered at the scale of the challenge he had been set: a comment which put into sharp focus the skill and preparation of the Swedish challenge.

Compared to the measured way in which Raynor and Sweden went about their job, Britain's attempt smacked of the make-do.

Busby found that none of the players had met each other before the squad was first brought together, and was so underwhelmed by the general standard of play that he asked his United players to give up part of their summer holidays to help train the squad.

After two hastily arranged friendlies, Britain started their campaign against Holland. A bruising encounter followed and according to the journalist Bernard Joy, the best that could be said of Britain's performance was that they showed 'enthusiasm and vigour'. This team, it should be noted, represented the very best of Britain's amateur players. The Swedish amateur players, by contrast, were playing a game that was technically in advance of the majority of England's professional clubs at that time.

Geoffrey Green in *The Times* wrote about the merits of the play of the Swedish amateurs and state sponsored Yugoslavians in the final:

> ... straight forward frontal attack and the through pass, these Continental sides employ a system of infiltration ... it is cunning, intelligent and scientifically planned ... the ball is kept on the ground and the passes glide to players who have the wit to find the unguarded spaces ... [the Continentals] have added a skilful switching of positions in attack and it is this element of positional surprise and the unexpected change in the point of attack that makes them so difficult to contain in defence.

Sweden's first game was against a full-strength Austria, captained by a marvellous player, Ernst Ocwirk, a garage mechanic from Vienna. Raynor told his team that a good start would be imperative against such opponents. The players responded magnificently to the instruction, and within 10 minutes Gunnar Nordahl had put Sweden two up. The Austrians became frustrated as the game wore on, were reduced to ten men when one of their number was sent off in the second half, and Rosen scored Sweden's third goal after 70 minutes.

Three days later it was the South Koreans on the chopping block at Selhurst Park. There were shades of the debacle of 1936 in Swedish minds prior to the game. In the Berlin Games,

Sweden had lost to Japan 3–2. All minds were focused on making sure that there would be no repeat shock against Asian opponents. Gunnar Nordahl scored a hat-trick in a 12–0 victory to put Sweden in the semi-final and the next day Raynor, fearing over-confidence, increased training for the squad.

In the semi-final, Sweden were to meet Denmark. Denmark had been lucky to get the better of Egypt in the first round, achieving victory only after extra time, but they were to give Sweden a tough match all the same. Against Austria, Sweden had been the first to react: now Denmark took the early initiative, and within 5 minutes of the start of the game they could have been two goals up. Seebach scored after 2 minutes and moments later Hansen struck the bar with a powerful shot. However, after 15 minutes Sweden equalised with a bizarre goal. Nils Liedholm, standing in an offside position behind the Danish goalkeeper, thinking quickly, ran into the goal when Sweden were attacking so that he could not now be flagged as being offside. His intention was, no doubt, to join the game when the ball was next cleared by the Danish defence, but Sweden won the ball and attacked from the wing. Henry Carlsson then headed the ball over the Danish goalkeeper and straight to Liedholm standing in the goal. That goal knocked the wind out of Denmark's sails, for after that it was all Sweden. They scored twice more before the interval, took their foot off the gas in the second half, allowed the Danes a consolation goal and ran out winners by 3–2.

On Friday, 13 August 1948, Sweden met Yugoslavia in the Olympic final. It would be a controversial game, and played in a very un-Olympic spirit. Raynor's optimism led him to order champagne before the game. He even ordered a special kit for the final itself, both ideas presumably designed to focus minds on the goal that was apparently within easy reach, but Yugoslavia would prove to be dangerous adversaries.

The Times reporter, Geoffrey Green, commented on what he saw as the key difference between the two sides: Yugoslavia, he wrote, played too laterally but the Swedes seemed to be 'always moving forward'. Sweden once again took the lead in the first half an hour: 'Gren completed a lovely move in which the ball sped at bewildering angles between four forwards.' Suddenly, Sweden became wasteful and three opportunities to increase their single goal lead went begging. Finally they paid the price for this when Yugoslavia's Bobek smashed home an equaliser moments before the interval.

Five minutes after an interval, during which Raynor had no doubt railed against any complacency, Gunnar Nordahl scored, but once again Sweden settled back, lost the initiative and allowed Yugoslavia to get back into the game. It was at this period in the game that Yugoslavia had two strong penalty claims waived away by the English referee Bill Ling. In both incidents the Swedish defender committing the 'foul' was Bertil Nordahl, trained by Raynor to add more bite to his tackles. Bernard Joy, reporting on the match wrote that 'Bertil Nordahl was the offender on both occasions and he was lucky to escape punishment. The setbacks rattled the Yugoslavs, their behaviour got out of hand for a spell and they did not recover their rhythm.'

These decisions seriously upset the Yugoslavians. Zlatko Cajkovski and Miroslav Brozovic were both cautioned. There are even accounts that another player, Branko Stankovic, was sent off. Bertil Nordahl suddenly found himself a marked man. He was seriously injured after one full-blooded challenge and as he limped painfully to the bench Raynor described him as being 'white with pain'.

In the rush to throw him back on the field the Swedish sponge-man applied the bandage so tightly that Nordahl could only hobble along. Meanwhile Rosengren, the captain, was shouting at Raynor to get Nordahl back on the pitch as Yugoslavia sought to press home their advantage. Raynor ordered the doctor to remove the bandage from Nordahl's leg and told Nordahl, 'You'll be alright once you get back on the field – go out there and try.'

Bertil bravely and immediately threw himself into a tackle, and now won the ball and played it up-field. As the ball went to the wing, Bertil continued his run, and received the ball again in the Yugoslavian penalty area. A defender challenged him for the ball, and down went Bertil. For some he went down far too easily, but Bill Ling (the English referee) awarded a penalty even so. Bernard Joy later reported: 'It is true that Bertil Nordahl was bowled over, but the offence looked no worse than those committed by [Bertil] himself on the Yugoslavs previously.'

Gunnar Gren converted the penalty to make the score 3–1 but the mood of the Yugoslavians remained poor. Upon the final whistle a Yugoslavian official went up to Raynor, who offered his hand in commiseration. Raynor wrote: 'He spat straight in my face and said, "Ah, English referee, English coach. Communist [he said, thumbing his own chest]. It is bribery."'

As the Swedish national anthem echoed around a rapidly emptying stadium, the temperature dropped quickly. The overcast sky had made the late afternoon chilly. It was a moody, anticlimactic way to signal Sweden's only international triumph.

7

AFTERMATH

The Olympics were both an end and a beginning for Swedish football dominance. The end was presaged by the presence of agents from the professional clubs of Italy. The Italian FA, possibly as a result of the war, now permitted their league clubs to play as many as three foreign players in their teams, and agents travelled throughout Europe to find players. The London Olympics was the perfect shop window for them and of all the teams there, the Scandinavians – and in particular the Swedish team – offered the most splendid pickings.

The agents soon came to the attention of Raynor. Initially they told him that they were in London to sign the England international Wilf Mannion, at that time living 250 miles away in Middlesbrough, but once Sweden had shown their true colours, the agents were less ingenuous. They now made it clear that their targets were Henry Carlsson and Nils Liedholm, and their methods became quite brazen. Just before the semi-final against Denmark two of them gained access to the Swedish dressing room at Wembley where they cornered some players until Raynor hurried them out of the room.

The exodus of the Swedish players to Italy and to other professional league clubs throughout Europe would soon begin in earnest. First to go was Gunnar Nordahl, signed by Milan on 22 January 1949; his brother Bertil was next, signed by Atalanta. Raynor knew immediately what the future held: 'I went back to Sweden knowing full well that I was facing an up-hill fight if Sweden was to keep her place among the soccer elite. New players had to be found.'

The euphoria occasioned by the Gold medal in London led to an immediate surge of interest in football throughout Sweden. Taking advantage of the national mood, the national Association initiated a series of reforms which sought to tap into that enthusiasm and hopefully guarantee that young players could be found to replace those who were being lured away to the Italian First Division. These initiatives represented a new beginning for Swedish football, for it was via this enthusiasm that the seeds were now sown that would be harvested at the 1958 World Cup. For his part, Raynor fully supported these programmes.

The first initiative was for the Technical Committee of the Swedish FA to assess how football was coached in schools. All sports teachers in Sweden had to pass a basic football coaching course: Raynor was now charged with assessing and offering advice that would give practical significance to those courses. In the 1950s, Rous asked Raynor to provide a review of how the Swedes organised school training for *The FA Book for Boys*. He described training sessions consisting of running, skipping, games and PT designed to loosen up the players for more intensive exercises later. Individual coaching sessions on key skills were used to separate and group players. Then there would be 6-a-side practice matches; meanwhile, overflow players would be further instructed in basic skills while the practice matches were taking place. These players would then be drafted into the practice game and those who had played in the practice match already would be taken away from the game and instructed in basic skills.

Further afield, *Idrottsbladet*, a sports newspaper, began a national sponsorship programme for 12–15 year olds to undertake tests in kicking, heading, dribbling, ball control and running.

Those who passed the tests were awarded bronze, silver or gold badges and their schools provided with football equipment and facilities; the more youngsters the schools put forward, the more equipment they got. Even national 'keepy-uppy' competitions continued to be popular; Gunnar Gren had previously been a champion. In addition, each of the national league sides introduced intra-club knock-out competitions for boys in the Under-16 category, with the best players being picked for trial matches for the national league reserve sides.

Further impetus was added with the so-called Stars of the Future courses: held annually, groups of as many as 200 players would be put forward by their local associations, and once convened and individually assessed this number would then be whittled down to a manageable thirty to go on the course. Sven Axbom, who would play as the left-back in the 1958 World Cup Final, was selected to attend the 1948 course, while Sigge Parling, another member of the side in the 1958 final, attended the 1952 course. Axbom remembered, 'The first time I met [George Raynor] was at Bosön in 1948 when I was one of "tomorrow's men", who were taken from different districts. It was cosy and nice. He was wonderful to deal with.' Kalle Palmer, a star of the 1950 World Cup, also recalls these events, commenting: '"Tomorrow's men" was a good initiative. It was a spur to continue encouraging the game. Raynor's role there was to observe and assess and he would also give out marks.'

Once the squad had been reduced to thirty players the National association would organise mid-season internationals in which the national side would split into an 'A' international side and a 'B' side made up of the promising youngsters. Before the war, Sweden had experimented by playing two internationals on the same day and now continued this policy. After 1948 the practical significance of these B internationals became vital because it was during them that future international players could be tested at that level. From those matches the best players from the A and B teams would then be selected to form the national side for either the October or November internationals.

One of those selected, who graduated to full international honours after being trialled at B level, was the IFK Gothenburg winger Bengt Berndtsson. 'I first met George in 1951 in one of the Stars of the Future training camps,' he said. 'He was really friendly and a nice person. In September 1951 George went with the A international side to play Yugoslavia and I went with the B side to play Finland.' Berndtsson would eventually be selected for the A side in 1956 against England and would also appear in the 1958 World Cup finals.

The Stars of the Future courses also offered an opportunity for trainers and coaches of each of the league clubs to congregate, and in doing so they were naturally sharing ideas and thoughts on the way players were playing and the way the game was being played. Out of this it was Raynor who, presumably out of necessity, organised the regular meetings of the coaches, from which new players and new ideas were trialled. This was certainly one of Raynor's strengths whether the idea of bringing coaches together was a natural by-product of the courses or an idea generated by someone else, he viewed and exploited the meetings positively. He was not closed-minded to new ideas and initiatives while overseas and saw the virtue and opportunity for such ideas when he returned to the UK. When he did return to the UK those ideas were, however, treated with suspicion and curried limited support. In this respect Raynor was, for an Englishman at least, ahead of his time.

These initiatives meant that Raynor maintained a close association with youth development at the league clubs and was also able to cast his eye over any players who had not been picked up by league clubs, but who had come to the attention of the local associations. Furthermore, the Swedish National Association called on Raynor to spend time working with the league clubs in addition to his work as national coach. To begin with, this work was on a temporary basis, spending a week or a month with one club before moving on to another, but in Autumn 1947 he started working as the coach with GAIS, the league club from Gothenburg, and the first signs of Raynor's limitations as a club coach (as opposed to his triumphs as an international coach) started to show. Although GAIS finished sixth they were only 3 points off the relegation place.

From the autumn of 1948 until 1952 he was employed by the AIK club in Solna, north of Stockholm. One of the youth players at AIK in the late 1940s was a youngster called Kurt Hamrin. Raynor and Hamrin would share a life-time friendship and one that Raynor would refer back to when discussing the benefits of intensive training of young players. Kurt later recalled the impact of his first meetings with Raynor when the Yorkshireman would commit himself to his young charge: 'When I started out in AIK in 1949 [Raynor] was head of the youth section there. As a 14 year old I played as a right-winger, and I imagine he saw me as the kind of player he was when he played in England. He gave me special practice drills with crosses, corners and other things, and he was always very careful that everything got done right. When it came to getting me to learn how to cross a football, I was almost brainwashed by George. I have had the benefit of him teaching me all my life. Unless my knee was so bad that I couldn't play he would wake me up at three o'clock in the morning, drive me to the AIK training field and drilled me in crossing the ball again and again.'

A well-established club side in Sweden, it was hoped that Raynor's influence at AIK could help the side challenge Malmo, at the time the pre-eminent league side in Sweden. Having taken over halfway through the 1948/49 season, Raynor would have been quite content to get his side to within 4 points of Champions Malmo that first season. Furthermore, the season was one of personal triumph, as AIK won the Swedish Cup in July of 1949 and under his tutelage the national side went through the season undefeated.

The 1949/50 season was less successful. Raynor's preoccupation was with the World Cup in Brazil, particularly toward the latter stages of the season when he left for South America with the national side before the season had even ended. Once again AIK were victorious in the Swedish Cup, but in the league Malmo's dominance remained unchallenged, completing the season without defeat, a lordly 16 points better than 4th placed AIK.

During the following season, problems started developing both on and off the field. AIK players would later be critical of Raynor's training methods. According to club historian Anders Johren, the players felt there was an imbalance in method. There was, they said, too much emphasis on ball skills and too little on fitness. As a result the team found themselves tiring toward the latter stages of league matches and the club's form stuttered. Worst of all, however, was a decision of the Board to announce that at the end of July 1951 the club would embark on a month-long tour of the United States.

As Anders explained, this tour was a dream for Swedish amateur footballers at that time. What put the cat amongst the pigeons was the fact that with finances tight the club gave notice that only those considered among the best club staff would be selected for duty, along with those players who were being courted to play for the club in the following (1951/52) season. The mood of the players understandably turned sour and Raynor could do little to calm the situation or save the club which, for the next 6 games, following the announcement of the tour, sailed perilously close to the bottom of the league. Of those 6 matches AIK lost 5 and drew the 6th. Their final match, as fortune would have it, would be against Malmo, Champions once again, and undefeated now in 49 league matches stretching back 3 seasons.

Two clubs would go down that season. Kalmar FF had already been relegated. AIK now needed to beat Malmo by 2 clear goals to go ahead of Elfsborg to save themselves. The circumstances played into Raynor's liking for counter-attack. Malmo were continually on the offensive but AIK, furiously and frantically battling away, defended at every turn and were rewarded with a quarter of an hour to go when a long punt from Hannerz, the AIK inside left, found Eric Grubb, who charged between Malmo's captain Nilsson and their keeper Pettersson to score.

Unfortunately, it proved to be the only goal of the game and wasn't enough to save the club from relegation.

The club did not consider Raynor to blame for the descent to the Second Division. He maintained a cheerfulness that continued to ally him with his young charges. 'He was a very nice man, I liked him very much,' said Hans Moller, a youth team player at that time. 'He was a good trainer because he tried different things. He trained us to play "the English way" and when he was there he would walk around and give all us players a good comment and would tell us to play a certain way. "Hans, don't do it this way, you have to keep the ball more," he would say. "Keep the ball, and the forwards should be running in order to receive the pass."' Raynor finally left the club the following December after guiding them through to the winter break undefeated.

In terms of the national selection, Raynor had a much more successful time: indeed it could be argued that at this time he recorded his greatest achievement for Sweden when recording a victory over the Republic of Ireland in Dublin in November of 1949. That victory came off the back of a splendid season for Swedish football in 1948–49 when the national side maintained the mood of their Olympic success by going through a season of matches undefeated. This included two matches against England and Hungary in Stockholm. Those two matches were the last hurrah of the Olympic side; they also give a pointer to the type of game that Raynor encouraged – defensive possession quickly converted into an attacking opportunity, the use of ball winners, incisive through passing, passing to the man, and movement to create further opportunity.

Of the England game, Geoffrey Green, writing in *The Times* the day before, had identified the loss of Gunnar Nordahl from Swedish selection as a key issue but was aware of the danger to the English posed by Gunnar Gren and Henry Carlsson, adding, 'and they will have the support of attacking wing half-backs in [Kjell] Rosen and [Sune] Andersson'. It was a Swedish side still bristling with talent: 'One need not say too much at this moment, apart from the obvious fact that the England team face a very real proposition' he wrote. Of the Swedes, Green recalled England's 1947 Highbury victory, achieved, he wrote, 'because of Mortensen's supreme opportunism,' and continuing, '[Sweden] keep the ball on the ground, move it quickly, and they run into position intelligently, finding the vacant spaces, but whether they can finish accurately remains to be seen, and that of course is the final answer in football to-day.'

Billy Wright won the toss but took no note of the conditions; the summer sun sets low in the Scandinavian sky in May, and Wright had his men kicking directly into the sun. Green used poetic licence to castigate the deficiencies of an English side which spent half the game squinting into the sun, saying that they 'resembled men groping about in a darkened room' when faced 'with clockwork precision'. In the opening 2 minutes Roy Bentley had scuffed an attempt to lob Svensson, the ball was fed quickly to Gren who countered immediately, his pass split the defence open and Carlsson smacked the ball past Ted Ditchburn. On the half-hour mark, Gren, standing on the Swedish defensive third, started a 70–yard four-pass move which Jeppson 'slashed home on the run'. Then 5 minutes before half-time, Gren lofted a cross into the box and Johnsson emphatically volleyed the ball past Ditchburn.

For England the defeat appeared to hold no lessons: they would go to Rio inflated by an expectation to win the World Cup founded on nothing but their past reputations, bustling technique rather than astute tactics their only weapon. They simply no longer had the type of players who could have given them the edge. As for the Swedes, it is interesting to conjecture what might have been had the 1948 side been retained in their entirety for the 1950 World Cup finals. Against Hungary, in their next match, Sweden showed their resilience. Two down with 10 minutes remaining they shook the Magyars with a resounding finish to draw the game 2–2.

However, as time moved on so did the players. Sweden was rapidly haemorrhaging a number of their best players. The pace of change was so dramatic that by October 1949 only three of the players from the 1948 Olympics were still available for national selection. In addition to the initiatives of the National Association

Raynor was therefore thankful for the Press v International XI match that was held every year. This was particular to Sweden and was a trial game that was played between an International XI selected by the National Association and a Press XI who were picked by the reporters of the national press. Through this outlet stars emerged. The press match would precede the international season. Raynor reasoned that the game gave a perfect opportunity to those on the periphery of international selection to stake their claim with a performance against the best players in the country.

In 1949, one such player was a young inside forward from Djurgardens IF (a league club in Stockholm) called Hasse Jeppson and his performance in the Press match that year made him a certainty for the England international of May 1949.

In early June 1949, Sweden defeated a resilient Ireland in Stockholm by 3 goals to 1 in their first World Cup qualifier. The Irish fought so hard that the Swedish cheerleaders were regularly entering the field of play during the second half to gee up the home crowd. Davy Walsh, the West Brom centre forward, had given Ireland the lead before Sune Andersson's penalty and Jeppson's goal before the interval set up a 3–1 win.

By the time of the return leg in Dublin in November 1949 Sweden had lost Liedholm to AC Milan; Ireland had, famously, beaten England 2–0 in Liverpool and one can imagine that the wind was in the Irish sails.

Then, just at the right time, a new star emerged.

Kalle Palmer was a 19-year-old product of Malmo's youth programme, and had performed well against Finland in the same qualification group. However, the decision to play Palmer against the Republic of Ireland was made despite Raynor's initial reservations. He did not think Palmer was ready for the physical demands of international football. 'He was a mere slip of a boy – only 5 feet 6 inches high and just over 9 stone in weight – but,' Raynor conceded '[he had] a great football brain'. Raynor's initial reservations were clear: '[he] had not looked … impressive … He looked rather like a refugee from a famine with his thin legs and his 9 stone.'

Raynor was not the only one to doubt Palmer: 'Many people doubted my capacity!' remembered Palmer, interviewed in 2011. 'Most doubted me because I was so very small, they thought I had such a poor physique. But my technique and understanding of the game outweighed the lack of weight.' Just as he had with Kurt Hamrin at AIK, Raynor worked hard in isolation with Palmer on his shooting and passing – so-called 'pressure training'. The intensive training paid off: '[Just] at the right time, [Palmer] found the form I wanted him to find … he had a wonderful brain and that priceless asset of being able to play the ball to a colleague just before he was tackled.'

When interviewed in 2011, Kalle Palmer remembered the game in 1949 in Dublin with crystal clarity: 'The pitch in Dublin was pure mud. It had been raining for 48 hours before the game. There were no directions [given by Raynor] considering the circumstances. We were told only to fight to qualify with enough points for the World Cup.'

The Irish defence perhaps underestimated the danger posed by the slight Palmer. His three goals buried Irish hopes and guaranteed qualification to the finals. The second of the goals, before half-time, reputedly carried a degree of fortune about it, with a whistle from the crowd stalling the Irish defenders and Palmer taking advantage of their confusion to score. Palmer remembers it differently, saying, 'I did not hear a whistle signal from the stands.'

Impressive as that result was, the last game of the season – a return match in Budapest against the Hungarians – resulted in a 5–0 defeat. By that stage, however, the loss of the main bulk of the Swedish players overseas was being keenly felt. Just why the Hungarians decided not to participate in the Brazilian World Cup is as great a mystery as what they might have achieved there. Raynor, accepting defeat to a richly talented opponent, did not veer from his default position of analysing team performance over the result. The defeat simply confirmed to the players and Raynor that in spite of the confidence instilled by defeating Ireland, Sweden still 'had a long way to go'. That winter he set up a training camp in Boson. '[We] tried out new ideas and experiments,' he wrote. The idea was to plug the gaps created by the wave of emigration, and Raynor concentrated on the forward line more than anything else, spending hours pressure training on Hasse Jeppson's striking. In doing so, Raynor would throw the ball to Jeppson at different heights and speeds until the striker was proficient at converting each chance first time.

Over the next few months debate raged in Sweden as to whether the Swedes should rely on the players who had now been bought by the professional club sides of mainland Europe – at that time, Sweden did not permit professional players to be selected for the national side.

In the end the conservatives' argument won out: Sweden would rely on their home-based players. The review of 'possibles' into the World Cup squad continued through the winter of 1949, with Raynor benefitting with the emergence of yet another talent, Lennart 'Nacka' Skoglund.

A player of tremendous self-confidence, Skoglund had only just been signed for AIK from Hammarby in the Swedish Third Division but he impressed Raynor enough to include him on the AIK tour of England in November 1949. In England his impact was immediate, coming on as a substitute at Chelsea and hitting the post with his first touch and so nearly forcing an equaliser. An 'unidentified player wearing the number 13' wrote *The Times* correspondent, adding mischievously, 'He should have worn a different number!'

Like Palmer, Skoglund was a skinny specimen; and like Jeppson before him, had come to the fore in the annual Press match, this time in the 1950 game. He was irrepressible. Raynor likened Skoglund to Stockholm with 'what a Cockney kid is to London', noting that the crowd screamed whenever Skoglund had the ball and Skoglund loved it: 'I told him frankly that if he would settle down to work and train hard he would go places in the game.' While Raynor had no doubts as to the footballing ability of both Palmer and Skoglund, their physical deficiency was a fundamental concern. After all, here was Palmer, able to split any defence open with a through pass, and Skoglund, able to go off haring down the left-wing, but neither would win the ball in a tackle with the full-backs and both could easily be shouldered off the ball.

Skoglund was drafted into Sweden's only match in 1950 before the World Cup: a home tie against Holland. Also in the side was the Malmo centre half, Ingvar Gard, who Raynor used to fetch the ball for the likes of Palmer. Palmer remembered his teammate in the following way: 'Ingvar had a phenomenal physical condition. He could run any distance and never seemed to get tired. He was very good in team games. He was enormously strong and really a "ball getter".' Sweden beat Holland 4−1, and all three, Skoglund, Palmer and Gard, would be selected for the squad: however, 'When we got to Rio I discovered that, like Kalle Palmer at that time, [Skoglund] was good in ordinary internationals but not so good in World Cup matches.'

Palmer was obviously anxious before the camp, unsure as to whether he had done enough to be selected for the final squad but he also had other concerns:

I don't remember very much about the training camp before the World Cup at Boson. It was uncertain whether I was going to participate in the final team for the coming World Cup. I had been turned down when I asked for time off for the World Cup finals in Brazil. Doing my national service was more important than the World Cup according to the powers that be in the Defence Ministry in Sweden. Two days before travelling to Brazil I was given time off by the Defence Minister himself, Mr Vougt.

8

A STRANGE KIND
OF TRIUMPH

Perhaps to modern eyes Sweden's performance at the fourth World Cup, held in Brazil in 1950, was hardly one of unmitigated success. In 5 games the team lost twice and conceded 15 goals. Nevertheless, Putte Kock called it 'Raynor's triumph' and in some ways it was miraculous.

After the widespread 'purchase' of their Gold medal team, Sweden were not expected to qualify from their group, so the fact that they went on to get third place, finishing in the highest place of all the European teams, with a squad formed from reserves and youth players came as a considerable surprise.

In only one match were they outclassed, and had they held on against eventual winners Uruguay in the last group stage (they conceded 2 goals in the final quarter hour to lose the match 3–2) might well have forced a three-way tie for the title.

In the post-war years, attack predominated defence and Raynor's focus was no different in this regard than that of others. It was the attack that he had worked hardest at, prior to the competition concentrating on improving the shooting skills of Kalle Palmer and harnessing the speed and mental focus of Skoglund on the wing. However, it is interesting to note that Willy Meisl, the Austrian journalist reporting at that World Cup, wrote of Sweden's defence that it was 'almost impenetrable, the best at the tournament', so it really was an all-round team performance that helped them achieve such a milestone.

Sweden arrived in Brazil in better shape than most. They had flown from Stockholm on a multiple-stop journey via North Africa; although taking 28 hours it was still preferable to the trip that the Italians, who Sweden would play their first game against, had undertaken. The previous year Italy had been traumatised by the air disaster at Superga in which the Torino football club had suffered greatly. As a result of that, a decision was made that the Italian team would sail to Brazil rather than fly. In addition, the Italian National Football Association had, surprisingly, placed two men in charge of the squad. The first was virtually a deferential appointment, for it was the President of Torino, Signor Novo, but the second 'manager' was a journalist from Tuscany, Aldo Bardelli. The voyage was long and rifts and disagreements developed during the course of it, so much so that Novo finally dismissed Bardelli from his position and elected himself sole team selector. By the time the ship docked in Brazil the players were travel-weary and tempers were short.

In the meantime, Sweden's decision to travel by air had allowed them time to settle in well before the games began. It was decided to first stay in Rio before flying the 200 miles down to Sao Paulo for the first game: a decision not favoured by all. 'The hotel in Rio was good,' remembers Kalle Palmer, 'but the location was difficult on the 3,000m tall mountain. We had a bus for long transport to our training [ground] and I felt the location of the training site was far too isolated.'

If nothing could be done about the distance from hotel to training pitch, other things, such as the food that the players were to eat and the training that they were to undertake, could be planned and prepared. Raynor had some involvement in contacting a Swedish émigré in Rio to help prepare Swedish dishes for the players. Training, meanwhile, was regimented to adhere to the demands of the climate. Early morning and late afternoon training sessions were held to avoid the heat during

the day: sprinting in the morning, a siesta and then match play
incidents in the afternoon; and vitamin C injections were given
where players were in need.

Training took place at Fluminense's ground, with Raynor
getting the players to run part way up and down Corcovado
Mountain as a warm-up. Other than that, training was kept
as light-hearted as possible – so much so that two Rio-based
European sides, Spain (from Pool 2) and Yugoslavia (in Pool 1),
came to watch the frivolities and see Raynor referee wrestling
bouts between the players which kept the players toned and
acted as a needed distraction.

Sweden's preparations were other-worldly compared to England's.

The Football Association had followed Tom Whittaker's
advice (gained during Arsenal's post-season tour of 1949) and
decided to base themselves at the Luxor Hotel slap bang on the
beach front at the Copacabana Beach. The area was notorious
and dangerous.

Charles Buchan's (the ex-footballer turned reporter) hotel
room was robbed while he slept. Firecrackers were thrown at
the feet of Bill Riddings and Jimmy Trotter whilst out on a night
stroll. And the hotel food was so impalatable that Mortensen
found himself consigned to a diet of bananas. One would have
hoped that the FA learned their lessons. But twenty years later
in Mexico the FA still based the team in a city-centre hotel
before their group match with Brazil in Guadalajara. That night,
car horns blared as the locals deliberately kept the English side
awake into the early hours.

Back to the fourth World Cup, and the Swedish team were
not favoured – primarily because they were amateurs playing
against the top Italian professionals. Furthermore, the fact
that the game was being played in Sao Paulo appeared, on the
face of it, to be handing home advantage to the Italian side
since the town was largely settled by Italian migrants. Indeed,
Willy Meisl, attending the game that day, reported that there
was a 'veritable drumfire of rockets' when the Italian players
entered the field; in contrast, Sweden emerged 'in silence'.

Raynor's antipathy toward the way the Italians had gone about denuding Sweden of their best players was evidenced in a statement he made after the game. 'We knew we could beat them,' he wrote, 'for I have never subscribed to the view that Sweden must always be the underdogs.' The plan therefore was to not be overawed by the opposition, but to attack.

Italy were ahead inside 10 minutes, with Carapallese scoring from close range when Capello crossed from the right. However, by the half-hour stage Sweden had taken control. Jeppson equalised, and then Sune Andersson put Sweden 2–1 up at 33 minutes in, after Skoglund had got to the byline on the left-hand side of the box. Sentimenti, the Italian goalkeeper, punched away the cross and Andersson, following up and under no pressure from the Italian half-back line, calmly controlled the ball on the right of the area and shot accurately through the crowd and into the left-hand netting. It was a goal which would have looked familiar to a pre-war Gigg Lane crowd when Ernie Matthews was arriving late to one of Raynor's right-wing crosses.

After the break, Jeppson, following up Palmer's shot from the right, corkscrewed the ball into the goal to make the score 3–1. Sweden were fortunate to hang on in the final minutes after Muccinelli scored a consolation. In the final minute Carapallese beat Svensson in the Swedish goal but the ball struck the bar and Sweden held on to win 3–2.

Meisl wrote that Sweden's was 'a truly excellent performance' and one warmly applauded by the sporting crowd. The result was the first of a number of shocks that characterised that World Cup and Meisl wrote that 'few experts had been prepared for [Sweden] actually beating Italy'. It certainly put the Swedish players in the lime light, not least Skoglund who became the centre of considerable speculation which no doubt affected the spirit positively within the camp.

'The swaying corn-cob' as he was called, with his glaring blond hair and peculiar running style, Skoglund became a crowd favourite and after the match a Sao Paulo club official even went so far as to approach Kock and offer US$10,000 for Skoglund.

That offer was refused but the one from an agent representing Internazionale of Milan following the competition was accepted. Inter offered US$50,000 for Skoglund! 'Mona Lisa [Skoglund's nickname] was the perfect team player,' remembered Palmer. 'He had a fabulous sense of humour, and he was respected by everyone. He was well into the game and had a desire to win which was infectious. He handed out praise and less kind remarks with a warm [even] hand.'

Paraguay were Sweden's next opponents. The game was played at Curitiba where the weather had turned very cold. Worryingly, Sweden again allowed their opponents to come back into the game when the result should have been assured. Sweden were 2 goals up after 25 minutes but finally had to settle for a draw. However, the draw gave them enough points to win the group. They now faced Brazil, Uruguay and Spain in the final group of the competition, the winners of which would be crowned World Champions.

The Brazilians had approached the competition with great preparation but the Brazilian Association had spent more time getting the personnel, tactics and the team right than they had in completing the stadiums.

How history would repeat itself.

That the team was strong was without question. After watching the opening Brazil v Mexico game, Arthur Drewery, the England selector, wrote: 'So much of [the Brazilian] game was baffling, but what impressed me most was their play without the ball. This, I think, was the main key to their success.' But they were subject to the expectation of the Brazilian people.

Huge pressure had come to bear on the team, and the side, though excellent, had shown that the weight of expectation could unnerve them. They had managed only a draw with the Swiss in their 2nd group match, although the Brazilian press castigated the referee rather than the team's performance.

In Brazil's next match, against Yugoslavia, they won but this time it was widely accepted that the referee had come to their aid. The stadium was still being built, and when one of the Yugoslavs (Mitic) injured himself on an exposed girder in the tunnel, the Welsh referee refused to show any discretion and blew to start the game while Mitic was still being treated. By the time he entered the field, Brazil were one up and only then would they go on to win a very tight game 2–0.

Raynor committed his mental resources to working out how to defeat them. Without doubt, the nervy manner in which Brazil performed came to the attention of Raynor and he felt it was a weakness he could exploit.

He explained as much to Sir Stanley Rous, who he met following the tournament in England. 'In the circumstances I just wasn't sure about Brazil. I kept thinking how nervously they played against my team until they got on top – we had two chances to score before their first attack.' And then he added, presciently: 'At the Maracana with all that expectation bearing down on them, I thought Brazil might struggle to find their best form against a team that wouldn't be intimidated by the atmosphere.'

This is exactly what would happen in the 'final'.

His attitude to coaching a team at that time was not geared to what we might nowadays understand as 'containing' their opponent. 'It is against my usual principles [to commit to defence],' Raynor wrote in his autobiography, 'For I firmly believe that the successful team is the team which dictates the play, the team which plays as it wants to play and makes the opposition follow.'

He felt, perhaps naively, that to put attacking pressure on Brazil would be more fruitful than trying to deny them defensively – and having the courage to attack Brazil was indeed the proper way to manage the threat as Uruguay were to demonstrate in the final decisive game of the competition, when they won 2–1 to take the title. But to beat Brazil, chances needed to be taken and mistakes avoided, something which Sweden were unable to achieve that day.

During the Olympics in 1948, Raynor had toyed with the idea of getting an early advantage over his opponents by scoring early and setting the pace. Once again his plan was to start brightly and take the game to Brazil. He later said that Sweden had two chances 'before Brazil even moved', one of which saw Palmer hit the post.

Without disrespecting Palmer, one can only imagine what Raynor would have given if Gunnar Nordahl or Nils Liedholm had played and had the same chance. Brazil survived and recovered. In the 17th minute Svensson got down too slowly to an Ademir shot that crept in close to the right-hand post: after that it was an avalanche and Sweden simply could do nothing to stop the Brazilians.

Willy Meisl wrote that he was impressed by the back line of Sweden's defenders (Andersson, Nilsson and Samuelsson, the right half) as well as centre half Sune Andersson (which gives some indication as to where the main action in the game took place). He was also impressed with Skoglund, who Raynor now brought into the inside-right position and played as his G-man. Although Meisl accepted that both Swedish forwards and the keeper made significant mistakes during the game, he went on to state that a 6–2 scoreline to Brazil would not have flattered them!

He then went on to write of Brazil that 'it must be put on record that we rarely if ever have watched such football artistry, matched by efficiency, as the home team exhibited. It was near enough perfect soccer.' The second half was purely academic, and Brazil ran out 7–1 winners. Sune Andersson's penalty brought Sweden some consolation but it was a contentious decision which allowed them to get on the score sheet – Juvenal's foul of Andersson was definitely outside the box.

Spain, the victors over England, had meanwhile started their final group matches against Uruguay and were unlucky not to come away with a victory when Varela rescued a point for Uruguay in a 2–2 draw. Seeing how Sweden had fared against Brazil the Spanish let it be known that they could beat Brazil. Brazil would beat them 6–1.

Sweden would now travel back to Sao Paulo from Rio to face Uruguay, but this time faring much better. Uruguay played with the same 'Bolt' formation and style of play of Rappan's

Switzerland, which Raynor had previously encountered back in 1946 during his first game in charge of the Swedish team, when Sweden won 7–2.

Sweden dominated the first half. Raynor had instructed his wingers to start sending over high crosses to test Paz, the opposition goalkeeper, who had been selected in front of the senior choice, Maspoli. Within 5 minutes of the start Sweden were a goal up when Palmer controlled Mellberg's lofted cross and struck his shot past Paz, the Uruguay goalkeeper, for a shock lead.

Uruguay got back into the game but their equaliser carried a degree of fortune about it with Ghiggia's shot being deflected over the reach of Svensson – who had been sound up to that point – to bring the scores level. Almost immediately, though, Sunqvist put Sweden 2–1 up: Paz utterly miscalculated the high cross into the box and Sunqvist took his chance well to give Sweden the lead again.

As the game wore on so it became more and more evident that Sweden's exhaustion was starting to tell. Egon Jonsson was injured in a challenge with Gonzalez, reducing their numbers and further increasing the threat of the Uruguayans.

In the 77th minute Miguez scored at close range to bring the scores level at 2–2. Then with just 5 minutes remaining on the clock Miguez corkscrewed a shot into the empty goal after Svensson had committed himself to a cross he could not reach.

It was a close game. Willy Meisl remarked that Uruguay 'had ... a hair-breadth escape'. Perhaps the constant travelling had finally caught up with the Swedish players: due to withdrawals from the competition, Uruguay might have been the fresher side, having had to play only one game in their group; maybe the second-half injury sustained by the Swedish player Jonsson in a tackle by Gonzalez played a significant part in the result – in those days no substitutes were allowed, so Sweden played the last half an hour a man light. Whatever the contributory causes, once again Sweden had allowed a lead to slip.

For their last game, in Rio de Janeiro, much was done by Spain to unnerve the Swedes. In their group match against England, they had employed all manner of dark arts to aid victory: now their tactics included just as much brinksmanship, but beginning before the game even started. On their return to Rio, Sweden returned to the hotel they had stayed in when they had first arrived in the city. Spain, not having given much forethought as to where they should base themselves in Rio, now decided that nowhere else would do to stay but at Sweden's hotel.

Whether this was a deliberate ruse to upset their famously placid European neighbours is hard to tell, but the Spanish challenged the Swedes to various parlour games and, Raynor remembered, beat them in the snooker competition. This only added to his resolve to make sure that on the football field Sweden would end on a high.

Raynor now gambled on resting Skoglund, putting Rydell in the centre-forward position and moving Mellberg to the inside-right position. He then swopped Jonsson and Sunqvist on the wings so that Spain, expecting Skoglund to play, were caught unprepared. As it transpired, Sweden utterly dominated their fancied opponents. Spain simply had no answer to the wing play of Sweden, with 2 goals coming from breaks down the right and Sweden creating enough chances to have scored 6. Sundqvist opened the scoring when Eizaguirre spilled a shot by Gard. Sundqvist's shot after half an hour was also converted by Mellberg in the goal area. Sundqvist again crossed for Palmer to score the third after 79 minutes. It was only then, when the game was secured, that Spain came back into the game. Zarra, the scorer against England, snatched a consolation goal near the end but the 3–1 result was a fair reading of the game.

Sweden finished in third place: Raynor could not restrain his glee and who could deny him? In a competition featuring the professionals of Yugoslavia, Italy, Spain and England, Raynor proudly announced, 'We became the No. 1 nation in Europe.'

9

THE DEBACLE
OF 1954

Following the performance of the team in Brazil, Sweden's players were once again the subject of major interest by the professional clubs in Italy, France, Spain and, in the case of Hasse Jeppson, who went to play for Charlton Athletic, England. Noting that as many as ten of the 1950 World Cup squad were signed up by professional clubs abroad, Raynor commented: 'We had just one forward and not one half back, but we were prepared to start once again.'

Amazingly, Sweden did come good again, due mainly to the organisational acumen of the Swedes and the wily stratagems introduced by Raynor, from which he was able to get water from an increasingly dry well. One of his preferred techniques during practice games was to purposely place players in different positions to their usual ones. He noticed that doing this took the pressure off the players; but it also allowed him to assess their hidden strengths.

One of the 'finds' using this tactic was the conversion of Bengt Gustavsson from club inside forward to an international-class centre half, a position that had been difficult to fill since the departure of Knut Nordahl to Roma in 1950. Gustavsson's debut actually came with a defeat in Copenhagen in 1950 but he would go on to become a mainstay of the international side that would make it to the World Cup Final in 1958. 'Mr Raynor was a popular trainer and trained us in the English way,' said Gustavsson, when interviewed in 2011. 'His training method was playful and his tactic was always to use the full width of the field with "blind passes" [by which he meant cross field passes to teammates making blind side runs] from the centre.'

Playful though those training sessions were, the underlying feeling was that Sweden's opportunities on the international football field were becoming increasingly limited: circumstances dictated that the side was constantly in transition and in the period between the Brazilian World Cup and the Helsinki Olympic Games in 1952, new players were being introduced with each match for the Swedish national side. Raynor's role was to find 'the right balance' within the team that he had left – during his tenure, he had lost the equivalent of two international squads and was now creating a third from scratch.

In late 1951 the Orebro inside forward, Ynge Brod, came to the rescue. His arrival, Raynor said, 'transformed the whole situation as far as I was concerned', and came just in time for the 1952 Helsinki Olympics. It soon became apparent, however, that the key was to find the right partner for him up front so that the team could make a worthwhile defence of their Olympic title.

Three warm-up matches were organised before the Olympic Games. The first was against France in Paris, March 1952, where the forward Westerberg played and scored a late winner; the second against Holland in May in Amsterdam (during which Brod was selected) resulted in a 0–0 draw; and during the final game, against Scotland in Solna, the team suddenly gelled and saw off the Scots 3–1 after taking an early two goal lead. It was 'a performance that gave me the key to our future success,' wrote Raynor, 'and made me certain that we could win a medal in Helsinki'.

Against Scotland, Brod's strike partner was Lars Erikssen but on further consideration Raynor and the selection committee eventually felt that the best candidate for the job would be a much older player, Ingvar Rydell. Rydell was the

Malmo forward who had been a 'squad' player during the 1950 World Cup, appearing only in the final match with Spain, despite having been the leading scorer in the Swedish domestic league during that World Cup season. Now, however, he would come fully to the fore and prove himself the perfect choice for the forward position.

To prepare the team Raynor was typically meticulous. He made an early sortie to Finland to ensure that the accommodation was agreeable, and even had a gate especially erected at the back of the accommodation so as to facilitate access to the training facilities. Then before the games themselves, the squad travelled to northern Sweden and to Boson, where the onus was on creating a good bond between the players. What made his job easier in this regard was the fact that the national selection committee had decided to take only a squad of twelve to the Olympic Games.

In the competition, Sweden started the ball rolling against Norway, winning 4–1, with Brod and Rydell contributed 3 goals. Against Austria they had more difficulties: 1–0 down to Herbert Grohs' strike before half-time, the score remained so until with just 10 minutes to go, the Swedes finally got into their stride and struck 3 goals past the Austrian keeper for a 3–1 win. Again Brod and Rydell contributed goals, this time 2 of them. That left Germany, Yugoslavia, Hungary and Sweden in the pot for the semi-final draw. 'If we got the luck of the draw … I felt certain that we would win at least the silver medal,' wrote Raynor. 'But the luck went against us and we met Hungary.'

The 1952 Olympics was the first international competition at which the famous Hungarian side – the 'Golden Team' – had been seen in the West. They had very quickly captured the eye of the commentators in Helsinki, already scoring 10 goals on their way to the semi-final. Raynor had taken the opportunity to study them following Sweden's quarter-final victory over Austria. A day later Hungary had met Turkey along the Baltic coast from Helsinki in the town of Kotka, and – even without the services of Nandor Hidegkuti, their famous inside forward – well and truly hammered the Turks by 7–1.

Despite the fact that Sweden had twice met Hungary in the previous season what Raynor now saw of them convinced him that the Hungarians had developed beyond all recognition. 'Hungary,' said Raynor, 'were just about the finest side I had set my eyes on', and Bernard Joy later elaborated on the way in which they played, writing:

> Hungary stressed mobility and interchangeability. No man was a slave to his position, but an all-rounder capable of playing almost anywhere. Although the long pass was not discarded, Hungary realised that short ones could be made more accurately, and so the players had to move within reach of the man in possession. The team advanced in waves, with players gathering around the man with the ball like the circles around a pebble dropped in water.

Hungary had achieved an exceptional run of results because of their teamwork, high technical standards when players were controlling and passing the ball, and because their players had the intelligence to position themselves so as to effectively support the man in possession. Confidence bred success. From May 1949 until the semi-final of the Olympic Games, Hungary had played 21 matches, scored exactly 100 goals and had lost only once. Hungary were determined to convert those results into Gold.

For Sweden to beat Hungary it would clearly take more than relying on the skill of the players because in all departments Hungary were far stronger. Reverting back to his experiences in the World Cup, Raynor once more toyed with the idea of starting quickly to force the Hungarians into a panic. Raynor explained his idea to Bernard Joy after the match. Joy wrote that Sweden 'banked on scoring a quick goal and then concentrating on defence'.

However, this plan, here, was undone by the referee, of all people. For some reason he kicked off earlier than expected, catching Sweden unawares. Hungary seized the initiative, scored first and by half-time a further 2 goals had already ensured their victory. Hungary went on to win 6–0. This caused Raynor to consider how best to prepare players prior to kick-off. One idea was to reduce the time between warm-ups and the game itself. He envisaged a situation where the players would go straight from pre-game training into the game not allowing for that period when the players troop off to the dressing room and fix their outfits. This would lead, he thought, to a cooling off period which could go against the team. Raynor conceded that the idea was only 'excellent ... if you can kick-off straight away'.

Hungary fielded a side that engendered fear and respect but it also brought into question whether its state-sponsored basis was in keeping with the Olympic ideals of the time. Their form of state-sponsored 'amateurism' could not be compared with the true amateur attitude that Sweden exhibited. Indeed, the final between Yugoslavia and Hungary was called the 'professional' final and the third-place match between Germany and Sweden was called the 'amateur' final. Whether it was a final at all, Sweden won it and once again Rydell was in the goals, scoring once in the 2–0 victory.

Although the 1952 Olympic Bronze must be counted as a success, it was to mark the beginning of the end not just of further aspirations but also, temporarily, of Sweden's partnership with Raynor. 'My work in Sweden hadn't gone unnoticed' wrote Raynor in his book; 'Italy ... had been trying to lure me ... for some time.' Although Raynor's version of the story was that his son initiated the move south (communicating back to the Italians that if the Italian clubs were serious then dad would only go there on the same terms and conditions as had been offered to Gunnar Nordahl. Evidently they were!) the main factor precipitating his move was Sweden's humiliating failure to qualify for the 1954 World Cup in Switzerland.

Even accounting for the loss of Brod (signed by Toulouse at the start of the 1953/54 season) hopes had remained high that Sweden would once again qualify for the World Cup finals when the draw pooled them alongside Finland and Belgium. Sweden's biggest opponent appeared to be that of over-confidence. After all, Sweden invariably got the better of Finland in their annual matches and Belgium, though boasting a team including

Pol Anoul at inside left, the well-regarded winger Lemberechts and centre forward Mermans, had shown no more than patchy form in the previous few seasons.

However, within the space of three days in May 1953 the group was effectively settled. Having beaten Finland 4–2 on 25 May 1953, Belgium then proceeded to beat Sweden 3–2 in Stockholm three days later to record a shock win and send them right to the top of the table. Sweden had even managed to let slip a 2-goal lead when losing the game, but worse was to follow.

In the away leg to Finland, Sweden were lucky to get a 3–3 draw (with another 2-goal lead for Sweden being wiped out) and only a Nils-Ake Sandell equaliser in the second half saved the side from yet another embarrassing defeat, and thus handed qualification to the Belgians.

Aware of the limitations of the side, Raynor was forced to continue to mask the reality of the weak standard of his side. 'We had to think of cute tactics to use at throw-ins, free-kicks and such set movements. But cuteness will not put you on top' he wrote. The elimination was a disaster. For the first time in three major international competitions Sweden would not be participating in the final stages; furthermore, as the National Association eventually decided not to enter the 1956 Olympic Games qualifiers (their attempts to lure Raynor back falling on deaf ears), it meant that Sweden's next competitive international fixture would not take place until the group stages of the 1958 World Cup.

The gloom would be permanently lifted in a tour made by the national side to Spain and Hungary which was undertaken in November 1953.

It was during that tour that Raynor put into practice an idea designed to ruffle the Hungarians and one that produced one of the biggest shocks in football history. Following the 6–0 defeat to Hungary in the semi-final in Helsinki, Raynor had set his mind to working out the weakness in the Hungarian team and he settled on a plan.

Sweden were not expected to do well in either match. Spain had been easy winners over Belgium that year, and particularly in the second of the games, away to mighty Hungary, it was widely accepted that the Swedes would do well to keep their opponent's score down to a respectable figure.

One of the players who was selected for the touring party was Kurre Hamrin, who had made his first team debut for AIK that May and by October was earning his first cap in the final 'dead rubber' qualifier to Belgium. A splendid winger, Hamrin would go on to play with great success for AC Milan in Serie A and in the European Cup and would give real strength to Sweden in the 1958 World Cup. Now, in the friendly in Budapest, he would surprise Hungary with his pace and energy.

Putte Kock, when writing about the tour, wrote that Sweden thoroughly surprised themselves against Spain and were unlucky not to win the game. He felt that Spain's equalising goal appeared to be offside but even so, Sweden could feel utterly satisfied with their performance.

For the second game against Hungary, Hamrin was drafted in. The Swedish squad were travelling light up front: the loss to the professional ranks of Eriksson and Arne Lundqvist brought the tally of international-standard forwards whose services had been lost to Sweden up to twenty-one. The committee and Raynor had no option but to rely on relatively new players. Seven forwards were now used in the two games, none of whom had more than two year's international experience.

Following the Hungarians' Olympic title in 1952, Sir Stanley Rous had arranged for England to play a friendly with them at Wembley in late 1953. As the date drew nearer, so British interest in the Hungarian national side increased; such was the curiosity that a number of English journalists and officials from the Football Association – including Walter Winterbottom – travelled to watch the Hungary v Sweden game which was played in Budapest on 15 November 1953.

The journalists sent over were John Graydon, at that time working for the *Sunday Graphic* but later head of ITV Sports, Desmond Hackett (*Daily Express*), Roy Peskett (*Daily Mail*), Clifford Webb (*Daily Herald*), and John Camkin (*News Chronicle*).

Geoffrey Green of *The Times* also reported on the game, which was the first friendly international not involving a British side to be featured in a full match report in that newspaper.

There is an apocryphal story that Raynor told one English journalist in Budapest that 'if we win I'll paint Stalin's moustache red', meaning that he would climb one of the statues of the Russian leader in Budapest and deface the icon, but whether he said such a thing at all is debatable.

Perhaps a member of the British press tried to construct an image of a man taking the task in front of him lightly or of mocking the Swedes, but Raynor knew well that the match provided him with a splendid opportunity to raise his profile in England.

When questioned, Raynor explained that 'the key-man was the deep-lying inside forward, Nandor Hidegkuti'. He added that his plan was to use a zonal marking system. He later explained: 'Our players had to stay in their zones and whenever Hidegkuti entered their zones, they were responsible for looking after him.'

Was it a sign of confidence to publicly reveal beforehand what he was asking of his team? Whatever the reason, he put his inside left on Hidegkuti in the first half, and then, in the second half, when Hidegkuti moved to the centre, left that marking job to John Eriksson, the Swedish centre forward. Such tactics would have been unthinkable in England. In England the forwards of the time, Mortensen, Matthews, Sewell, Robb and Taylor, would have found it perverse to have been asked to mark and help defend.

Raynor's attacking instructions are not known but it is interesting that he argued that the Hungarians were not strong defensively. What is curious is that no one else had even considered any similar tactic before to confound the Hungarians, and none would make similar inroads into combating the Hungarians until the Germans upset the odds to beat them in the World Cup Final the following summer in Switzerland.

John Eriksson, the Swedish centre forward that day, remembered Raynor talking to each of the players in their hotel room in Budapest before the game, confirming his instructions to them individually. When it came to the 6ft 1in Eriksson, who

Raynor had nicknamed 'the big elephant', he just told him to be strong in the middle.

Afterwards he expounded the zonal plan to the British journalists in greater detail, explaining that the Hungarian wingers purposefully played deep in order to coax the opposing full-backs to come out of position to find 'their' opponent. It was this action of holding the ball, pulling their opponents out of position, that allowed the Hungarians to exploit the gaps in their opponent's defence and so dominate the games in which they played.

Raynor now planned to turn the tables and do to the Hungarians what they had done to every other side. Raynor instructed his own wingers to mark their opposite number and gave firm instructions for the defenders, particularly, to hold their position when Hungary had possession. Raynor also instructed his players to counter-attack.

These were novel ideas but when the game began, it was typically one-way traffic for Hungary. Sweden found themselves holding on.

The Times noted two characteristics about Sweden's first-half performance: 'boundless enthusiasm' and 'vigorous defence', observing that Sweden put 'up a defensive screen of between eight and ten players' which wasn't surprising given the fact that Raynor's men were marking opponents in attacking positions.

In the first half, Puskas and Bozsik both hit the post and, according to *The Times*, no less than six further chances went begging for the home side. From the press box Sweden looked defensive, but it was effective defence and represented a relaxation of Raynor's belief that the best way to play was to impose your own tempo on each game.

At half-time the score was o–o.

During the interval, the Hungarians withdrew Sandor Kocsis; bringing on Peter Palotas. Hidegkuti now moved to the centre-forward position.

In the 50th minute, Puskas missed a penalty after the Swedish defender, Samuelsson, had handled the ball. Puskas pulled his kick wide, and would, later, write of the trauma as he saw his kick fly past the goal in his autobiography, momentarily overcome with fear that his failure would lead to defeat. Now it was time for the Swedish to turn the tables. Ten minutes after Puskas' miss, Palmgren, the Swedish inside right, shocked the crowd when he put Sweden one up.

They were unlucky not to keep their lead. Two minutes after Palmgren's goal, Palotas, freed by Hidegkuti's pass, struck a shot past Svensson, the ball hitting the post on the way in. Sweden were still very much in the game when Tibor seemed to clinch it for Hungary when he put them 2–1 ahead with barely 12 minutes to go. Once again Putte Kock felt the goal was offside from where he was sitting in the stand.

Perhaps Hungary, believing that the match was won, relaxed. If that was the case, they were extremely lucky to get any type of result out of the game, as Sweden did not drop and started to attack the Hungarian full-backs. Suddenly the invincible Hungarians looked vulnerable. With 5 minutes to go Hamrin, coming in from the right-wing, scored to make it 2–2. Then with only moments to go in the game, Hamrin again stole clear of the defence and let fly a tremendous shot which beat goalkeeper Grocsis but the ball, agonisingly, struck the bar.

Years later, the Hungarian centre half Josef Bozsik described the sense of relief that the referee's final whistle gave to the Hungarians and also the double benefit which the draw provided for them. The result 'shook [us] out of a growing complacency ... [also] it probably made England over-confident. For instance, the *Daily Express* reporter [Desmond Hackett] wrote there was no reason for England to fear the Hungarians, and that Britons could safely bet on an English victory.'

Never had a British coach and journalist done England a greater disservice.

The match details are as follows:

15 November 1953, played at the People's Stadium, Budapest, Hungary, in front of 80,000

Hungary: Grocsis; Buzansky, Lorant; Lantos, Bozsik, Zorias; Buzs, Kocsis

(Palotas), Hidegkuti, Puskas, Tibor.

Sweden: Svenson; Samuellson, Gustavsson; Bergmark, Svenson II, Hamrin, K. Jacobsen, Erikson, Palmgren, Jacobsen F.

0–1 Palmgren ('60); 1–1 Palotas ('62); 2–1 Tibor ('78); 2–2 Hamrin ('85)

After the game, Gustav Sebes, the Hungarian coach, cornered Raynor and asked him to highlight any negatives he saw within the Hungarian performance. Raynor noted that the wingers were more geared toward attacking rather than doing the unglamorous spadework when seeking to get back, support their defence and start the attack again. 'I told [Sebes] that although both Hungarian wingers came back deep now and then to try to draw the Swedish defence, neither came back into contact distance quickly enough when a Swedish attack broke down,' wrote Raynor. 'By that I meant that if the [Hungarian] outside right moves forward and loses the ball, which is cleared [by the Swedish defence], the [Hungarian] outside right must immediately come back very quickly to make contact with his own defence so that he will be ready for the short pass when the defence gets possession.'

According to Raynor the Hungarians corrected this part of their game when they played later that month at Wembley and it is interesting to read the quote attributed to Hidegkuti in *Inverting the Pyramid* prior to the game at Wembley: '[Sebes] decided to ask the two wingers to drop back a little to the midfield, to pick up the passes to be had from Bozsik and myself and this added the final touch to the tactical development.'

This may or may not amount to the same thing; certainly, Raynor was advising that the distinction between the attack and the defence needed to be corrected, because for the wingers to do nothing but attack would be to make the work of the defenders unnecessarily onerous. They would, after all, have to pass the ball longer to their attacking colleagues than if those colleagues were inclined to 'track back'.

In Budapest, against Sweden, the Hungarian defence had been somewhat isolated by their own wingers and midfielders and this had allowed the Swedes opportunities to run at the defence rather than have to battle for the ball in midfield.

News of the draw was discussed across Europe. The lessons learnt that day were not lost on the likes of Sepp Herberger and Helmet Schoen, the German coach and trainer. Raynor stated that he was not overly impressed by the Hungarian defence, and Schoen picked up on this when he later said, 'If the Hungarians had a flaw it was that because of their unbroken sequence of success, they only wanted to play and not to mark.'

Raynor believed that if England could take a leaf out of Sweden's book and adopt the same zonal marking game, then it was certainly possible that they could win the match at Wembley:

> I am convinced that playing in the old British style and spirit England's footballers can win at Wembley on Wednesday. England's opponents are weak in defence but have a strong, clever forward line. Their key man is centre forward Hidegkuti. The Hungarian forwards are extremely good at passing and inter-passing and fast at re-positioning. England must win to maintain the prestige abroad of fellows like myself.

What did Raynor mean by 'the old British style and spirit'? Presumably he felt that if England were to play in their own dominating style, and really take the game to the Hungarians and not play into the trap that Hungary would set them, then England did have a chance to win. But England would need also to be flexible to the challenge being presented to them, contain and pressure the Hungarians when they had the ball just as Sweden had done.

After the match between Hungary and Sweden, Raynor had a chat with Joe Mears, the Chelsea chairman and head of the FA's International Selection Committee at the time. Raynor explained the tactics that he had used against Hungary and suggested that England do the same at Wembley.

Mears nearly choked on his post-match tea and biscuit exclaiming, 'Can you imagine me asking Stanley Matthews to go in and challenge Czibor?' He told Raynor bluntly that England simply did not have the players to adopt the tactics that Raynor had used against Hungary. This could be interpreted in two ways: either the players were not skilful enough to adopt a zonal marking system, or they were so arrogant that they would not subvert themselves into some demeaning system of containment.

According to Billy Wright, both the Swedish and the English contingent flew back to Austria together, and it was there that Walter Winterbottom, the England manager, and Raynor sat down together in a Viennese café on the Monday morning following the game to discuss the lessons learnt.

Winterbottom quizzed Raynor on what would be the best plan for the England v Hungary match coming up, and listened to Raynor's views that England should not fall into the trap that the Hungarians had set up for all their opponents over the years.

Raynor made it clear that the one thing Winterbottom certainly should not do would be to detail the centre half, Harry Johnston, to man-mark Hidegkuti because to do so would give opportunities for the Hungarians to have players and possession into the gap that Johnston would be vacating. It should be noted that since Raynor saw Hidegkuti as 'the key man' he would hardly have restricted his advice at that point. Presumably he would have advised on a similar strategy that he had employed: that is to zonally mark the Hungarians when England were not in possession; in other words, to detail one of the forwards to have marked Hidegkuti, leaving Johnston to read the attack in the centre of defence. To English ears and imagination this would have been difficult to comprehend because their football had become so prescribed that any deviation would have left them bemused.

Wright wrote that Winterbottom ignored Raynor's advice. Winterbottom was, according to Wright, 'too deep a soccer thinker to judge any team on one display when things did not quite work out for them'. Was Wright correct? Did Winterbottom really ignore the advice? The answer to that question is that he partly followed the advice given by Raynor but otherwise ignored it. What do I mean by this? Winterbottom, according to Brian Glanville, later said that before the game he offered Harry Johnston, England's centre half, 'the option' as to whether he would like to go track Hidegkuti (i.e. applying the third back game) or remain back in defence (i.e. Raynor's idea).

Johnston himself wrote (in his autobiography) that he told Winterbottom he wished to remain back in defence and that left Hidegkuti to play much further up the field against England than he would otherwise have played. In other words, Johnston chose to follow Raynor's suggestion. A viewing of the 1953 game certainly supports Johnston's position on this. He was regularly to be found in England's penalty area.

(It is interesting to note that when England went to Budapest the following year (and Syd Owen was selected in place of Johnston) Owen marked Hidegkuti conventionally which opened the door for an even worse result for England.)

However, Johnston was only one link in the chain, albeit an important one. To an English way of thinking the third back was an auxiliary defender upon who rested the responsibility of repelling the chief attacker. Whether teams were successful or not in stopping the centre forward normally equated to whether the centre half had done his job. The problem with this, of course, is whether the opponents are playing to the same plan. It benefited England nothing if Johnston played in the centre of defence and Hidegkuti was not otherwise being picked up by one of the English forwards. To have issued instructions to one player, therefore, and avoided debate with the others allowed Hidegkuti the freedom to roam around the English midfield, hit off a shot when in range of goal, or set up his inside forwards when the opportunity arose.

Mortensen, Sewell, Robb and Matthews were certainly not detailed to press and mark any opponents when Hungary had the ball. Watching film of the game, it can be seen that wing players like Matthews and George Robb are to be found in the centre of the English half of the field but that was not on the basis of some devised plan. That was because the ball was mainly to be found in that area and they were forced to congregate into the centre of the field to win back possession.

Constrained by the reluctance of his players, Winterbottom therefore could not introduce the type of tactics Raynor could utilise and English football got taught its famous salutary lesson.

It was a defeat that simply left the nation bewildered. Following the game, First Division managers were all called to attend a meeting to discuss lessons learnt. Stan Cullis, the respected Wolves manager, had highlighted his own bemusement when he harangued Walter Winterbottom's use of Bill Johnston and asked why Johnston had not been detailed to mark the Hungarian No. 9? Winterbottom reduced this enquiry to absurdity. If the Hungarian left-back had worn No. 9 would Johnston have been better employed marking him?

For Raynor it was confusing. 'What the reason was for England refusing to listen I don't know. It could have been a wave of pessimism had struck the FA and victory had already been conceded to the Hungarians. Or it could be that a powerful nation like England with immense resources was too proud to learn from little Sweden.' He maintained considerable suspicion that nothing would have changed in England had they lost that next week by one or two goals. As it was, they were annihilated 6–3 but even then, the only changes instituted by the Football Association were bizarre.

In their bemusement the FA introduced various initiatives, but they were cosmetic. There was a decision later taken, for instance, to change the playing kit of the England team. Out went the collars, and in came a new-style v-neck top. Out went the long shorts, in came less baggy shorts.

The Wembley result clearly indicated that Raynor had got his sums right.

10

ITALIAN
INTERLUDE

Raynor continued to coach during the 1953/54 season at Atvidaberg, a small municipal team in the Second Division in Sweden. At the end of the season they undertook a tour of Germany during which Raynor received further correspondence from the agents of Juventus of Turin to ask if he would be interested in managing their side. Raynor saw the offer to work in Italy as an opportunity to test himself in a highly competitive league. The lure of the lira was also as strong a pull as the opportunity to work amongst the best players and coaches in the world:

> When I got back [to Sweden after the Atvidaberg tour of Germany] there was not one but two Italian agents there to meet me. One represented Lazio and the other Torino. They made all sorts of offers in their efforts to outbid each other, and in the end one of them agreed to act as my agent as well as the agent of the club he was representing. (That is how they work things in Italy. Even the agents have agents!)

Raynor had already made his mark on Italian football by coaching Sweden to international success: the Italians, freed by a decision of the Italian FA to sign foreigners after the war, had attracted the best Swedish players to their clubs. Nils Liedholm and Gunnar Nordahl were still playing for Milan, while Hasse Jeppson, after a short period with Charlton in London, was now at Napoli, and another Swede, Arne Selmosson, was at Udinese, now coached by the Hungarian, Bela Guttman.

At Roma the coach was a fellow Englishman, a Liverpudlian called Jesse Carver. Like Raynor, Carver had also been a middling professional footballer before becoming a coach of great renown. Carver had been the Dutch coach during the 1948 Olympics in London, where the high expectations of them had been disappointed when they went out in the first round. Carver exhibited a worrying tendency throughout his career: part way through any agreed term, he would jump ship. He did so with the Dutch FA, would do so again in the early 1950s with West Brom and later with Coventry City too. Notwithstanding this, he was always in demand. He had actually won the Italian Championship at the first attempt in 1950 with Juventus, but after leaving Italy for England had returned to Italy and was now earning a king's ransom at Roma and living with his wife in Via Archimedes, alongside Ingmar Bergman and King Farouk, in the Eternal City.

Carver was a crafty, cautious character, traits that protected him from the type of Italian football politics that would easily upset Raynor's much more trusting personality. Brian Glanville called Carver 'a self-contained, circumspect figure' who reporters would only hear from when criticism was levelled at him by the press. It was a persona that Carver clearly imposed upon his wife: she would be the one who would squirrel away packages of cash over the border in Switzerland, and who was discouraged by her husband from offering any type of hospitality to the expatriate community. She would invite Glanville or Raynor back to the Carver's place for Sunday lunch, only to then have to feed them an excuse about having to see a dressmaker in order to avoid welcoming them into the apartment. 'The amount of times I heard about that dressmaker,' Raynor ruefully commented.

Raynor clearly did not have either the time or opportunity to scrutinise Carver's mindset in those early months, but he would have done well to study it. As he was to discover, Italy was a thoroughly alien environment. Sweden and Britain – even the Iraq of the war years – had simply not prepared him for the chicanery that he was to discover in the Italian football. Carver, meanwhile, knew implicitly how best to play and treat the local press and, more importantly, how to keep the club directors on side as a result.

When Raynor first arrived in Italy he was astonished by the largesse of Giovanni Agnelli, the patriarch of the great Fiat car-making empire. 'Really I was in a daze,' he wrote. 'My mind went back to the days when I hadn't got two halfpennies for a penny. And yet here I was, standing alongside a millionaire and pointing out the car I would like. To me it seemed incredible.'

From the off Raynor was sold the idea that he would be given a long enough time with Juventus to put his slippers under the bed. It is unfair to knock him for being so trusting; after all, Agnelli did come across as being a man of his word and gave Raynor a verbal assurance that the contract would be for two years. The professional demands of the game in Italy, however, did not permit years of building and development: the game there, founded on the parochial small-minded rivalries between a handful of sides from the three principal cities, required immediate success. By way of example, Bela Guttman, a coach of great knowledge, got the sack at Udinese after just 11 games in charge during that season.

At Juventus, Raynor made a reasonable start, only losing 1 game in their first 6, but by mid-October of 1954 they were already 5 points adrift of Milan. A 1–1 draw with Catania immediately sealed Raynor's fate, and he was 'loaned' out to Lazio, the club side from Rome, and at the time bottom of the league with 3 points from their first 8 games. His analysis of the ailing team was candid: 'Lazio at that time were not successful, and after I had seen the lads train and play I realised what was wrong. Basically, the team selection had been completely haywire … But I came up against a problem I had never met before and never want to meet again … I began to hear rumours of a practice I never believed existed in football – bribery.'

The shock to Raynor may have been instant; what he decided in the circumstances was to impose himself on team selection. Brian Glanville, who worked in Italy during the 1954/55 season, wrote that Lazio had placed their transfer policy in the hands of Gigi Peronace, an agent but also a significant presence in Italian footballing circles of the day. Peronace had brought in Parola and Giovannini, two elderly defenders; little wonder that Lazio started the 1954/55 season by shipping goals to all-comers. It must have come as a complete shock to Raynor to find a professional club being led by nothing more than an agent. For Raynor it was just another example of the extraterrestrial world he had entered.

There was a further hindrance: Count Vaselli, one of the owners of the Lazio club, was opposed to Raynor even being there, and – given the populist power of the moneymen within the game – the press clearly sided with the local owner rather than the foreign manager. This reflected the reality of football in Italy: the owner governed the club, paid bonuses and, as a result, had the ear of the players, while the manager was just a short-term expendable. Considering all this, what Raynor achieved during that season was miraculous: 'Lazio,' wrote Glanville, 'battled against relegation,' but the truth is somewhat different.

Under Raynor, Lazio became a competitive side, winning their way to a comfortable mid-table finish in his first season in Italy. Such players as John Hansen, the Danish international who had come over with Raynor from Juventus, and Gosta Lofgren, his Swedish international centre half and another of Raynor's G-men were excellent during the season; allies in a hostile environment.

Raynor's first challenge came in only his second game with the club, at an away fixture at Catania, and before which some of the club professionals openly warned Raynor about the amount of bribery going on. 'When such things come on the scene it is difficult to know what to do because it is hard to pin down the culprits. So I decided to watch and wait. I also decided to be tough with my team selection and leave out any player, however famous, with my team selection.' Lazio lost 1–0. Raynor certainly had his mind focused by the performance of the incumbent goalkeeper and when Udinese, still coached by Guttman, and featuring the Swede, Arne Selmosson – 'the Ray of Moonlight' – came to Rome the following week and beat Lazio 2–0 it was enough to convince Raynor to draft in the 35-year-old reserve goalkeeper Guiseppe Zibetti, for the relegation battle with Pro Patria:

> It was that decision which brought me face to face for the very first time with the fanaticism of Italian football. The newspapers called me crazy and demanded that I resign immediately … I realised that my reputation, maybe my life, rested on the slender thread of Zibetti, the goalkeeper I had chosen, having a good game and being so well supported that we not only avoided defeat but actually won. We won the match, and Zibetti ran up to me, crying his eyes out, and hugged me for joy.

After the turn of the year, Lazio produced a remarkable run of victories, beating Inter, Juventus, Fiorentina and Atalanta before playing Roma in the Rome derby. Following the match Glanville castigated Jesse Carver, the Roma manager, for getting his tactics wrong in a match which Roma should have won. 'Under drenching rain, John Hansen [the Lazio forward] stooped to head an early goal, and Lazio won, 3–1.' Raynor wrote of the Italian character revealing itself in the aftermath of the game:

> The Italian leaps to the heights of happiness in victory and … touches the depths of despair in defeat … he doesn't agree that the loser should congratulate the winner … as I found out after we had beaten Roma … Jesse Carver came up to me, smiling as any British manager would, shook my hand and said, 'Well done, George. You deserved it. The best team won.' Everyone in Roma said, 'It was all fixed to help Raynor.'

Following the game John Hansen, interviewed by the press in Rome, pledged his support for Raynor, but the line was suspiciously edited out of the final copy. However, there were signs that Raynor was beginning to get to grips with the nuances and 'morality' of Italian society as time crept on. Per Bredesen, the Norwegian right-side winger, was being seen in the bars and clubs of the capital so Raynor detailed a private detective to catch him 'in the act' and then threatened to tell his wife what her husband was getting up to when he next met the player.

It turned Bredesen's season around and ensured a successful run-in for Lazio. The side lost at Torino in March, but otherwise remained undefeated from early February until mid-April when they went to play Pro Patria, an inferior team, bottom of the league and supposedly heading out of the top flight.

It was this match that finally convinced Raynor that Italy was simply not for him:

> As each week went by I became more convinced that everything was not what it should be on the playing side … We were due to play Pro Patria … and three or four players … asked to be rested. With a full team the game should have produced [a win], but I noticed many members of the team were not obeying my … instructions. Eventually we got a penalty-kick … and the ball was rolled straight at the happy Pro Patria goalkeeper! To make matters worse, one of their players was sent off the field, so a few minutes later [Renzo Sassi] walked up to an opponent, kicked him and walked off the field to even the numbers.

Lazio finally finished twelfth in the Italian League, which in any other environment would have been an adequate completion to a first season, but Raynor was sick of the lies and deception inherent within Italian football and assaulted by the suspicion and lack of trust emanating from Count Vaselli and the fickle nature of the press. The ambivalent opinions he constantly expressed about England were momentarily put to one side when he compared the qualities of the respective nations:

'All I wanted to do was get away from Rome and Lazio ... I was desperately unhappy ... Let this be shouted from every rooftop in Britain – there might be a lot wrong with football in Britain, but there is no corruption.'

What happened next was astonishing.

11

COVENTRY
CITY

George Raynor's next move was as surprising as it was unexpected. After establishing himself in Rome and fighting to win over the club players and fans, he suddenly became a pawn in a remarkable story which took him from the giddy heights of Serie A where he was working alongside the best coaches and players in the world to the dugout at Highfield Road, Coventry City in the Third Division South of England's Football League.

Just how this came about requires an examination of the characters of Jesse Carver, who Raynor had met in Italy, and of the character of W. Erle Shanks, the owner of Coventry City Football Club, who successfully brought both Carver and Raynor to Highfield Road in the autumn of 1955.

Jesse Carver was at that time one of the best football managers in Europe, but had earned a reputation for leaving jobs halfway through contracts, normally when distracted by the promise of more money elsewhere. In the 1940s, he had infuriated the Dutch FA by walking out on their national side without notice or warning. Carver had already successfully coached in England in the 1952/53 season when he had been at West Bromwich Albion, and while there had introduced new ideas into training. Getting players to train with a football during the week was one idea that apparently caused quite a bit of fuss at the time, but it has been written that the success Albion achieved in the mid-1950s (when they came so close to winning the league and FA Cup double) was due in no small part to the work Carver had done while he was there.

The Albion directors, conscious perhaps that appointing him as manager would expose them to his overt interference in club affairs, kept him as a non-contracted coach and while the club prevaricated Torino came calling. He stayed a year at Torino and then went to Roma when a more lucrative salary was offered to him. Carver was a wily operator and one gets the impression that when they met in Italy, Raynor, with all his honesty and straightforwardness was really in a different league to his fellow expatriate. Brian Glanville described Carver as being 'buttoned up and closed. His smile was always knowing, rather than amiable.' However, for all his secrets and chicanery, Jesse Carver was at the top of his game in 1955 and those seeking a quick fix, like Erle Shanks, were quite content to overlook any shortcomings.

Coventry in the mid-1950s was a prosperous city. Jim Brown, the Coventry City FC historian comments: 'Coventry was still being rebuilt following the war but it was a boomtown in the 1950s what with the car industry and lots of people came to Coventry from all over the country because that's where the jobs were.'

High employment meant that people had more money to spend on leisure activities and the city was awash with post-war prosperity and abuzz with gala events, opening nights at the theatre, visiting Hollywood stars and civic pride. In the newspapers the city ladies were seduced by adverts in which models were glamorously paraded in kitten heels and Dior. Across town a huge conglomeration of bicycles represented the transport of a vast union rally, which urged pay rises for workers in the busy factories.

At the time, the owner of Coventry City FC was a timber merchant named W. Erle Shanks and he had big plans for the club. Jim Brown described Shanks as 'larger than life' and that he was never fearful of broadcasting just how much of a saviour he was to the club in those post-war years. He was always happy to talk to the local newspapers but when he did, invariably the subject was money. With a huge professional workforce being attracted to this hub of industrial Britain, Erle Shanks could see the opportunity for a well-supported club to climb up through the divisions and compete alongside the big clubs from Manchester, Sheffield and London.

At the time the maximum wage applied to professional football in England. In theory this gave all clubs a chance to succeed because it applied whether you were playing at Aldershot or Arsenal. Since clubs could not attract players by offering high wages, they found other ways of securing and retaining their men. In some cases, club chairmen and directors would co-opt players onto the payroll of the companies they owned, who were required to do little if any work to draw a secondary income to supplement their wage. Shanks employed a similar tactic at Coventry when trying to retain the services of Reg Matthews, the star goalkeeper at the club.

A quick survey of the league tables of 1956 evidences the way the maximum wage acted as a real leveller in the game. In the First Division, small town clubs like Blackpool, Burnley, Luton, Cardiff, Preston and Huddersfield competed alongside Arsenal, Manchester United, Everton and Aston Villa. In those days clubs still had opportunities not just to 'survive' in the top division but to really establish themselves. In that same year, Leeds United and Liverpool were both Second Division teams, while in the Third Division Ipswich Town had just employed Alf Ramsey.

In 1955, Ipswich, like Coventry City, were in the Third Division.

Within seven years they would be competing in Europe as Football League Champions.

The general air of prosperity in Coventry may have fostered similar ambitions for Shanks to think big for his club but during the 1954/55 season Coventry City were in disarray. In this regard the club was in familiar waters because in the early 1950s, Coventry City had experienced a tumultuous period in

their history. In 1953 they had their lowest gates since the 1920s, lost
their manager Harry Storer in November and seen their directors
resign en bloc. Jack Fairbrother had come in from Peterborough
to take over the managerial reins but he only survived until
October 1954 when ill-health had forced his departure.

Lol Harvey, one of the players at Coventry at that time,
remembered the disaffection felt by the players that season.
'We were having a bad time before Jesse Carver and George
Raynor came. Charlie Elliott was the acting manager at the
time and there was a tremendous fuss in the dressing room after
one of the games when Charlie was in charge. There was open
mutiny in front of Erle Shanks after that game because some of
the older players were saying 'but we haven't got a manager!'

At the end of the 1954/55 season Coventry City finished 23
points down from the top spot. Shanks became determined to find
a new manager to take the club forward. Not only did he want
Coventry to get promoted to the First Division, he also wanted
them challenging for honours. For whatever reason, Shanks
decided that the manager Coventry needed to do this was Jesse
Carver. Shanks' desire to bring Carver to Coventry certainly
supports the view that he had massive ambitions for Coventry City.

In November 1953 the *Sunday Graphic*'s John Graydon,
surveying the devastation of England's 6–3 defeat to Hungary,
had stated unequivocally that there were two ways that England
could regain their power in world football – by bringing George
Raynor and Jesse Carver back, and placing them both in charge
of the national team. One cannot know whether such an article
played on the mind of Shanks, but in 1955 he went to Rome
armed with nothing more than his plans and a cheque book and
met Jesse Carver.

The audacity and success of taking Carver from the highly
paid sophistication of Serie A to the Third Division South was,
in my opinion, the biggest story in European football that year.
During their meeting Shanks revealed his plans for Coventry.
At the time Carver was still the manager of Roma, who he had
coached to a third-place finish, achieving the double over that

season's champions, Milan. Was Shanks persuasive or was Carver
wily enough to use the opportunity to secure himself a better
deal later in Italy? The question is easier to answer when we
examine the contract that Carver was now being offered. Shanks
could not match what Roma were paying Carver, who was
reportedly receiving £5,000 per year. All Shanks could provide
was a salary of £3,500 per year for the next three years and a
house in Borrowell Lane, Kenilworth.

Money was always a pre-eminent issue for Carver. Although
he may have had other reasons for walking away from the bright
lights and glamour of Serie A, knowing what Carver did when
he eventually returned to Rome in January 1956, one is half
persuaded to surmise that by accepting the appointment to
go to Coventry City, he would be freed from his contract at
Roma. He may have known that it was likely that he would
become the subject of a bidding war between the other clubs in
Italy to secure his services, for this is precisely what did happen
in December 1955 when Inter and Lazio emerged as the two
principle contenders for his services. On his return to Italy he
was offered more money by the smaller Lazio club than he had
previously been on by Roma. Make no mistake, Jesse Carver
was a very wily operator.

There are only a few details of the meetings between Shanks
and Carver that we can be reasonably clear about. One is how
much Carver was being offered, and the other is that Carver
made it clear to Shanks that he would only come to England
if George Raynor was included in the deal. Carver clearly
respected Raynor's qualities as a coach; after all, in the Rome
derby in March 1955, Raynor's 'struggling' side had gone to
Roma and given them a comprehensive pasting.

Shanks accepted the proposal. All Carver had to do now was
to convince George Raynor that the Third Division South was
where it was 'at'. Raynor knew nothing about this meeting
between Shanks and Carver, but he certainly wanted out of Italy,
where he was receiving no support from Lazio's owners and
hated the corruption he was finding there. In his autobiography,

Raynor states that after accepting Shanks' offer, Carver employed the services of his devoted wife Emilie to convince Raynor's wife that George should join him at Coventry. Nevertheless, Raynor had already been thinking about working in England: 'I decided it was time to try my luck in England and was just on the point of getting in touch with [some] clubs when my wife met Jesse Carver's wife. His wife told my wife that he would like me at Coventry City as coach.' As a result, Raynor was quite happy to throw in his lot with Carver and had idealistic visions of what the two could achieve together.

On his return to Coventry, Shanks broke the news to the players. Lol Harvey remembers, 'He told us that he had appointed Jesse Carver and George Raynor. We were in amazement. But, he said, they can't start until the start of the new season.' Over in Europe, once it became common knowledge that Carver and Raynor were leaving Italy, the Swedish FA apparently contacted Raynor on the off-chance that Raynor would once again perform his magic in forming a side for the Melbourne Olympics in 1956. The Swedish FA allegedly offered Raynor £2,000 to take the job for the next year – but here was the opportunity which George Raynor had desired for so long: his chance to work professionally as a coach in England. It was far too good to refuse. Sweden didn't send a team to Melbourne, but importantly the respect for Raynor in Stockholm remained; that same year, 1955, Putte Kock included a chapter on George Raynor in his book *Fotbollen – Mitt Ode* (*Football – My Destiny*).

The decision to take the job was hardly the easiest appointment Carver and Raynor could have undertaken. The Third Division South was not a division lacking in talent. In 1956, Coventry's talented young goalkeeper Reg Matthews was asked to write an article for that Christmas favourite of old, *The Big Book of Football Champions* entitled 'Give the Third Division its Due'. In the article he refers to the many players from the Third Division – John Atyeo, Geoff Bradford, Peter Sillett, Frank Blunstone and Dennis Wilshaw – who within a few years had all established themselves at international level.

Not only was the Third Division South a place for great finds for those clubs in the higher divisions, it was also a place of education for ex-player coaches like Peter Doherty and Raich Carter. Matthews had been one of two reserve goalkeepers at Highfield Road and now found himself promoted to first team football by Carver. More astonishing still, during the 1955/56 season Matthews was called up to represent England in the Auld Enemy clash. He started the season playing for the England Youth side and was then selected for the Under-23 and B internationals before his senior call up in April 1956. He was to retain his place against Brazil at Wembley and for the Continental tour that summer before Chelsea secured his signature for £20,000 in time for the next season. His promotion to the first team was one of the key decisions of Carver's reign.

On 16 August 1955, just days before the start of the 1955/56 season, Carver, who had been on a scouting mission to Scotland, returned to Coventry and was greeted by banner headlines as to what he had allegedly been up to. Typically, he sought to avoid any publicity: 'Since I've been away there have been several reports of what I was going to do. They appeared without my knowledge and if I had been here would not have done so.' It was a quote redolent of an intentionally secretive man.

That same week, having assessed the playing staff, Carver, on Raynor's advice, sold Coventry's other reserve goalkeeper, Peter Taylor, to Middlesbrough. It was a smart piece of business and would change the course of English football history because while he was at Middlesbrough, Taylor would befriend the 20-year-old centre forward Brian Clough.

Clough and Taylor, of course, would achieve success by winning the Football League title with Derby County and Nottingham Forest in the 1970s and take Forest on to two European Cup titles in 1979 and 1980.

The arrival of Carver and Raynor at Coventry immediately amazed the youthful Lol Harvey, astonished at the Continental changes that they instituted into Highfield Road:

When Raynor came along, we all had our feet measured for clogs. We were then measured for our training kit and match kit. And before training it was all hung out for us. It was wonderful. Before this our training kit was normally thrown on the central table in the dressing room. It was awful. You'd all dive in and the shirt wouldn't fit, the shorts would be too big, the socks would be odd. George was a wonderfully friendly Yorkshireman. Perhaps he was too friendly to be a football manager. But if someone was having a bad time he would always put his arm around them. He was totally different from the men I otherwise worked under.

The difference between the two was also quite obvious for Lol who got on well with Jesse Carver:

Carver was a very shrewd man. He was a clever man. He seemed to know everything money-wise. He went back to Italy for the money. But when he was at Coventry he was always in the background, always standing on the touchline. Before training George and Jesse would get together and decide what was going to happen. I went to visit Carver in Bournemouth years later. He had a flat down there. His wife ran the whole show.

In terms of the training the impact was just as immediate:

[Carver and Raynor] changed everything when they arrived. All I knew before they arrived was running around the track, maybe a practice match on Tuesday morning but then on Wednesday we would have road running. When they arrived we had to report to the training ground at Cotswood at 10 a.m. If you didn't you were fined. And then we trained with a ball. George organised a league and we played in 5-a-side matches. Each side had a team name and it was really competitive. And George also got us to play on hockey pitches. It was all about passing, passing, passing. At one point I remember he put his arm around me and said, 'Lol, when you haven't got the ball keep looking around so that you know where you've next got to pass the ball.' I was only a young lad of 18, but it was all about ideas with George.

Pre-season expectations went through the roof.

Season ticket sales at Coventry in 1955 were the best since the war. The season began with a triumphant home win over Bournemouth in front of 24,000 people. As Jim Brown went on to write: 'The football was slick and exciting. At home Carver's team were unbeatable but away from home they struggled for results and promotion hopes looked slim.' It didn't stop the dreams of the supporters though. Buoyed by the initial success of the side, Shanks offered a bonus option to the players through Raynor. The players would get £20 per match if they attracted over 16,000 through the turnstiles or £20 per match if they could get the team into the top four. 'We went for the gates,' said Lol Harvey. 'But Raynor instilled confidence into us, and told us, "Look lads, you've made a mistake. Go for the top four!"'

Just imagine, 20,000 people packed on the terraces at Christmas 1955 watching their local club playing utterly sophisticated Continental football and with two of Europe's top coaches in the dugout. It's a romantic image but it really happened. The playing fortunes of the club, however, remained inconsistent. By October 1955 Coventry City had gone 8 home games without defeat, but by the same date they'd had a run of 7 away games without a win. Carver went to Shanks, convinced him to part with £5k and gave it to Reading for the signature of inside forward Dennis Uphill. In November 1955 Carver went back to Shanks and asked for the cash to sign Ken McPherson who was out of favour at Middlesbrough. The results of Uphill and McPherson's arrival at Coventry were immediate. With Uphill's support, McPherson was instantly amongst the goals. Newport were defeated 3–0, and Millwall beaten 5–1.

One felt that now the club fortunes would in time turn, the squad would establish itself, and Coventry progress forwards. Lol Harvey remarked of the period: 'God, we were going places! The club was buzzing. We were amazed and the fans knew what was coming.'

The problem was that Carver, forever leaping rafts mid-stream, was now being sounded out by Internazionale in Milan. Sensing that a big offer was about to be made, Carver started telling

Shanks that his wife was not well and was considering cutting short his stay in the Midlands, but kept back the news of Inter's interest in him. When he found out, Shanks was obviously livid and made it quite clear to the press as to his feelings.

On 31 December 1955, in the same month that he had brought McPherson to the club, Carver handed in his notice. What the Inter officials expected was that Carver would now come to work for them. However, on Boxing Day 1955, Lazio contacted Carver and offered him £130 a week (approximately £5,500 a year). Inter were fuming when they realised that Carver would be flying into Rome rather than Milan. The Inter spokesman was curt and abrupt when the reporter from the *Coventry Evening Telegraph* contacted them about whether they had struck a deal with Carver before Lazio; the phone in Milan was reportedly slammed into its cradle. A few years later Carver wrote: 'When I left ... Coventry City in late 1955, I was contracted by [Lazio] ... Count Vaselli, presented my wife [Emilie] with a bouquet of red roses.' The Italy he was heading back to contained both the beauty of the roses and the danger of the thorns, but Carver always looked before he leapt.

12

THE LOW POINT AT
HIGHFIELD ROAD

On being quizzed about the reasons for Carver's departure, Shanks clearly wanted to avoid any suggestion that he had been forced to resign, making it clear that he had been given everything he'd asked for: 'Mr Carver has had an entirely free hand from the start. Everything he has asked for he has had. He has had a completely free spending hand. No one has interfered with anything. If he has asked for the moon he has had the moon.' The *Evening Telegraph* reporter tried to make sense of Carver's stay in the Midlands but concluded that Jesse Carver had looked decidedly out of place in the post, dressed in exquisitely tailored suits complemented by a healthy Italian tan, and with his decision to suppress his Scouse accent leading him to speak with a weird brogue.

Raynor now became manager but it was hardly a move he had desired or anticipated. The absence of Carver now created a vacuum the likes of Raynor could hardly fill. Whereas Carver was unknown, circumspect and no-nonsense, Raynor was the good cop, placing a reassuring arm around his charges, surveying the youth side with a view to encouraging and cajoling; a friend to all. In other words, he was not and would never be English football management material.

Given the type of boardroom personas floating around the main stand and the type of players ruling the roost in the dressing room at Highfield Road, it would have taken a far stronger character than George Raynor to have steadied that particular ship. He had come over from Italy almost in an advisory capacity; chief decisions being hammered out between Carver and Shanks. Now Raynor was being asked to place his hand on the tiller and plot a successful course. Unfortunately, Shanks' attitude towards Raynor was never a charitable one, and one suspects that he now had a manager he had never actually wanted, and did not know what to make of or do with him.

He had offered Raynor £1,000 a year for an initial three-year contract and agreed to provide a house for free – but then just as readily reneged on the offer of the house. The disparity in treatment between Shanks' wholehearted support for Jesse Carver and his lack of belief in Raynor did not take long to come to a head once Carver left town. The interference, missing when Carver had been in charge, now started in earnest.

Raynor's tenure began ominously. At the end of January 1956, San Lorenzo, an Argentinian side on tour in England, played Coventry. This was another coup for Shanks; San Lorenzo had otherwise been playing First Division teams and this was a chance for Coventry to join the international fever sweeping European football that year. Unfortunately San Lorenzo's trip coincided with a dreadfully cold, wet winter and their secretary, Alberto Marina, complained that due to the conditions of the pitches his players simply could not play as they did in Argentina and, presumably, the weather inhibited any sense of the expressive Latin joy.

The previous Saturday they had met Wolves at Molineux and were incensed when Mervyn Griffiths awarded Wolves a penalty in the home side's 5–1 victory. To the Wolves supporters the sight of players surrounding and pushing a referee added more belief to the impression one had of the Latin temperament.

The following Wednesday, at Highfield Road, San Lorenzo's players were at it again.

The game had attracted 17,357 to the ground and initially all seemed quite normal, with Coventry putting up a good fight when taking the lead through McPherson's goal after 28 minutes. This lead was then cancelled out less than 10 minutes later by Gutierez. Then, 2 minutes before the interval, Dennis Uphill hit the post with a shot and as he followed up to score, two San Lorenzo players sandwiched him so that he couldn't reach the ball.

Arthur Ellis gave a penalty kick.

Once again the Argentinians lost their composure and surrounded the referee. One of the players, 19-year-old Jose Sanfilippo, kicked out at Ellis, who immediately sent him off. The player refused to leave the field. Ellis called for assistance from two policemen and Sanfilippo struggled and kicked both of them as they tried to pull him off the pitch. Fearing that the remaining players would be similarly disposed, Ellis blew his whistle and abandoned the game.

Ever the businessman, Shanks' first concern was that the crowd would demand their money back. 'I almost went down on my knees to Mr Ellis, but he would not consider carrying on,' Shanks told the *Telegraph* the following day. The rules of the friendly stated that no substitute referee could be called upon, so in such a situation – unprecedented in English football up to that time – once the referee refused to carry on, the match had to be abandoned. Thankfully, perhaps agreeing with McPherson's own opinion that Coventry had got the better of Lorenzo, the crowd behaved impeccably and left without complaint.

Shanks met with the San Lorenzo staff to discuss the match with them. This was seen as a sign that bridges could be mended and in the following days the Argentinians made it known that they would gladly meet again for a further friendly, but Shanks was less keen. Uppermost in his mind was the question of whether the Coventry public would happily part with their money for a rematch, rather than any considerations of the inherent benefit to Raynor's men in meeting international opposition. As there were no guarantees, Shanks refused to countenance a return game, and although he did invite Spartak from Yugoslavia for a friendly in February of 1956 (to add more Continental flavour to the fixture list) the match never took place.

The Coventry job was never going to be one where the boardroom were going to grant Raynor time to develop any youth development programmes or develop some of the less effective senior professionals. The directors were anxious for the club to quickly advance up the league. Raynor had encountered interference at Lazio from above and now, at Coventry, he was to experience it yet again. Shanks had favourites at the club and rewarded them accordingly, while other directors simply assumed command since it was 'their' club and completely disregarded Raynor's wishes.

One such incident arose on 3 March 1956, when Raynor had gone to see a player at Scunthorpe on a match-day, leaving the team confident in the knowledge that they should easily be able to overturn a Crystal Palace side which was heading the wrong way out of the division. Unfortunately Coventry lost 3–1.

'When I returned the players told me that a director [Mr Robins] had gone into the dressing-room at half-time [at the interval Palace led 3–0] ... and played merry hell with the players ... I had an agreement with the directors that no one should speak to the players or criticise them. If any director wanted to make a criticism he would have his opportunity at our weekly meeting after I had given my report.' Very soon discipline at the club started to unravel, with Raynor remarking that the club spirit was 'provoking'. Players didn't seem to care and publicly challenged him, and in doing so undermined the team spirit.

All of this must have come as a complete shock to Raynor, whose previous experience in English football had been at a time when entrenched loyalty was a by-product of a period when a player dropped by his club might well find himself out of work and without access to the dole. When Norman Bullock had dropped him at Bury, Raynor had worked his socks off to get back into the first team. Now, imposing a similar penalty on players at Coventry was met with an arrogance that took the wind out of Raynor's sails. Coventry in the 1950s, with its prosperity and factories full of workers, was a vastly different England to the one Raynor had played and lived in during the depression of the 1930s. In cricket the literature had reflected this social change, whereas C.B. Fry before the war had penned *A Life Worth Living* now English society was more Dennis Compton's *The End of An Innings*.

One player who Raynor threatened to drop replied, 'All right, carry on and drop me. I can get fourteen pounds a week sweeping the floor in a factory.'

To modern eyes, such a statement from a professional footballer (let alone to a manager) would be incomprehensible, but in those days of the maximum wage, a player could quite easily earn his playing wage doing various manual jobs. Coventry was short of labour, with plenty of opportunities for work, and the players knew it. They also knew that Raynor did not have the support of the Board.

Lol Harvey's assessment of Raynor is quite interesting:

> George wasn't a manager. He was pushed into the job when Jesse Carver left. George was a coach. There wasn't a better coach anywhere at that time. But, as a manager, he didn't have what was needed. By way of comparison if you think of what Harry Storer was like, well Harry would get a call from the press about 'player power' at the club. Harry would say 'Well, I've no problem with that, as long as they know I'm charge, it doesn't matter about player power.' You see, Harry had the respect of all the players, no matter what they said. A manager has to have that when he takes over. George never really had that.

This, in a nutshell, is the essential paradox of George Raynor. In England, where football demanded management types who tolerated no backchat from players, Raynor was considered a pushover. It is odd, perhaps, that a former army physical training instructor of sergeant status should find himself unable to assert much dominance over a group of lower-league footballers.

But management of players and the appeasement of directors who had unsustainable aspirations was not Raynor's forte. In Sweden where the amateur ethos accommodated a much less dictatorial regime he had the ear not only of the top Swedish players but also of the upper echelon of the National Association's administrators. In that environment he was allowed time and opportunity to shape future planning with the general support of the clubs and administrators. Raynor's character perfectly complemented that forward-thinking philosophy.

In England, where hard-nosed commercial concerns predominated in the hurly-burly of league football, such issues as developing the club from the youth team upwards featured some way down the list of priorities (if it featured at all).

League football in England was, as it is now, all about increasing revenue for the clubs. It was about securing promotion by invariably bringing in better-quality players and securing larger crowds for higher-profile opponents. This was an attitude that Raynor was out of step with, for he realised that long-term such a view was simply not sustainable. The way to improve the strength of the club and to sustain success was to invest in youth, bringing through younger players and replenishing from the base up. Raynor wrote:

> It grieved me ... promotion to [the directors] was everything ...
> It was more important to them than solid progress ... Many directors
> are businessmen with no knowledge of the game ... I admire
> football-minded businessmen who climb the social ladders, but I detest
> those people who use football purely as the ladder.
>
> At Coventry I was gradually weeding out the bad players and the bad
> clubmen and organising my own youth development plan. But that did
> not satisfy the impatient. They wanted immediate results, and although
> the players were beginning to respond to my coaching methods those in
> charge would not wait.

Raynor was a talented coach no matter where he went. What he lacked, throughout his career, was an attitude which imposed an iron rule over those he managed; it was simply not his style to so conduct himself. Perhaps he was too set in his ways. Perhaps he had not the mindset and flexibility required to succeed in the professional environment of England. His unwillingness to be a bit tougher might have been his undoing in England but it had prompted success in Sweden, particularly where young players had been encouraged to graduate up through the ranks.

Not only was Raynor out of step with the attitude of the directors. He was also discovering that the club were not supportive of his attempts to impose order on the players. Disciplinary sanctions imposed by Raynor were not backed by the club. One player who clearly took advantage of the club rule allowing him full wages when injured in a first team game, malingered on the sidelines for a while and Raynor was forced into placing him on the transfer list at the end of the 1955/56 season. However, when Raynor got back from holiday the player had been taken off the list by the directors of the club without consultation with Raynor.

Not all the players were anti-Raynor – Lol Harvey and some of the younger players were happy to work for the betterment of their club – but although annoyed by their attitude, Harvey was powerless to stop those players who, as he called it, couldn't give a toss. 'The likes of me and a few more from the apprentices played their hearts out for the club; but this wasn't the same for all.'

In June 1956 Shanks, still unconvinced that Raynor was the man to manage Coventry City, persuaded Harry Warren, the Southend United boss, to come to Highfield Road. It was a move which further undermined George Raynor's standing. Warren's Southend had done well toward the end of the 1956 season but they had finished in fourth place, well behind Alf Ramsey's Ipswich in third place, and what's more had shipped nearly as many goals as they scored. It is probable that the reason Shanks brought Warren in for Coventry was that neither Brighton (who finished second), nor Ipswich wished to part with their respective managers at that time. Warren's arrival may well have signalled the re-introduction of Raynor to the position of club coach but it also meant working under the sort of club professional that had not the background to appreciate where Raynor was coming from.

The writing was on the wall, and Raynor approached Shanks in June 1956 and told him that he wished to resign before the new season began. Shanks called a meeting of the directors and they persuaded Raynor to stay in his position as chief coach to see how things developed at the club under Harry Warren. Whereas Shanks didn't think Raynor was management material he clearly had no problem with Raynor as club coach.

There were some bright spots in the gloom. In August 1956 Raynor found himself in possession of a giant of a man from South Africa called Stephens 'Kalamazoo' Mokone, the first black African player to ever sign professional forms in European club football. Promoted and financed by Charlie Buchan (the ex-England international and journalist) Mokone had attracted the interest of Newcastle United the previous year but his passage to England had been halted by his father, determined that Stephens should first complete his education.

Now, having got his qualifications, he was free to go. On his arrival in London's West End, Mokone visited the Fleet Street offices of his patron, Charlie Buchan, who took his protégé down into the courtyard of No. 408 The Strand, for an impromptu kick about! The following day Mokone travelled up to Coventry. Just why he picked Coventry was bemusing. When questioned by a newspaper reporter Mokone simply explained that he had seen the name of the club in a newspaper and thought he would give them a try. Photographed alongside Shanks and another director, Mr Hitchener, Mokone spoke pidgin English: 'People very friendly, but not the weather,' he replied to the inevitable press question. Mokone was then driven over to the Allesley Old Road, at the time known as Coventry's 'Africa Circle' – literally a place where black Africans lived in Coventry and where a resident of the area had been asked to accommodate him.

On 14 August 1956, a trial was arranged between the first team and the reserves and Mokone found himself in various one-on-ones with Reg Matthews. Mokone scored early on, selling the great goalkeeper a cheeky dummy when doing so. Later, however, a penalty was awarded and the ball was handed to Mokone. Lol Harvey, who played that day, takes up the story: 'When the penalty was awarded, the game was stopped and then there was this long delay because the press cameramen had to all go and position themselves behind the goal in preparation of the penalty. Mokone placed the ball and then retreated all the way to the halfway line to start his run up. Anyway, Steve came running in, right up to the ball … and missed! But he was a lovely man, was Steve.' Raynor said to the reporters, 'Mokone shows promise and masters the ball well … it is too early yet to tell but I think he will need building up physically before he is match fit. He flicks the ball in continental fashion but he must develop a more powerful kick.' In the end Mokone would play for the first team but only in less than a handful of matches before leaving England to play in Holland.

However, such moments of light relief were rare for Raynor at Coventry. Under Warren, the side were soon in a worse predicament than they had been under Carver. McPherson and Uphill, considered the cornerstones for an attempt on the division title, were showing none of the enthusiasm that had made them so feared the Christmas before. As soon as the season started the press began a campaign against the way the club was playing. The local press reporter 'Nemo' was savage in his criticism of the tactics of the team: after a 4–0 defeat at Northampton on 8 September 1956, the *Evening Telegraph* printed a story under the heading 'Football like this will never take City to Division 2' and went on to state that the absence of Peter Hill and Eric Johnson, 'sabotaged what speed and ability existed in attack, and there are no replacements.'

It was the performance of the team around this time that was the cause of so much concern. Results went in their favour but the nature of the victories pointed to fundamental problems at the club. On 10 September, Norwich were beaten 3–2 but only after a half-time rollicking from Warren inspired a comeback that wiped out a 2-goal deficit. Five days later, QPR were beaten

5–1, but 4 of the goals came in a late 8-minute spell; the first was clearly offside but allowed to stand, and Rangers, having lost their cool, collapsed. Against Ramsey's Ipswich things were no better in two back-to-back matches. An away defeat on 19 September and a pitiful 1–1 draw at home five days later led Nemo to really stick the knife in: 'A painful prolongation of wretchedly poor football, slow handclaps and ironical laughter.'

Behind the scenes the club was already starting to implode. Shanks went public with his support for Harry Warren and his backroom staff but within a fortnight Harry Barrett, the chief scout, was sacked. Shanks then had to face the press, denying that he had survived a vote of no confidence. Scenting blood, Nemo gave the knife a further twist after the team lost 1–0 at home to Reading on 29 September, writing, 'so low is the ebb of confidence now, that it took only a mediocre side like Reading to rub in the salt'.

Raynor now tried to offer ideas to Warren to arrest the slide but found that what might work with players of international class did not necessarily work with players in the Third Division.

Jim Regan came in against Torquay on 6 October at inside left and was expressly told to play as a G-man in the formation, deep-lying and passing quickly out to the wingers. It didn't work and rather than threaten Torquay the opposition easily soaked up the pressure and won 3–1.

At the turnstiles the crowd started to desert in droves. Shanks, spotting an opportunity to regenerate interest, told Warren that Mokone must play. Mokone was brought in to replace Alan Moore in the home game against Millwall on 13 October and reportedly added 5,000 to the gate, eliciting a great deal of fuss from the large crowd every time he touched the ball, but such a move couldn't stop the rot. Gordon Pulley's goal for Millwall particularly upset the crowd, because when the blond striker knocked the ball home Reg Matthews was lying injured in the penalty area. Millwall won 2–1.

At the end of October, four players were transfer listed, including Dennis Uphill, and on 9 November Reg Matthews also put in his request for a transfer. Warren called him 'a foundation stone for my team of the future' but after playing for England against Scotland in April 1956, Matthews, understandably, had been considering his options to leave.

On 5 November 1956, Raynor resigned and went to live in Skegness, where he had bought a property in October. The press challenged him about the reasons, suggesting that he had disagreed with Harry Warren, but Raynor was adamant that this was not the case. Raynor's beef was not with Warren but with the directors, who had reduced his role as coach to automaton status, prescribing orders for him to enact. He had followed these orders until it became too much to stomach.

Later, he accepted that he should have stayed and persevered, hoping that his ideas would eventually win out over the notion that short-term investment would bring long-term success: but at the time he felt that it was simply a rejection of the ideals and principles upon which he had formulated his success with Sweden.

Furthermore, the lack of faith the board had in him was mutual and without that confidence there was no point in devoting time and energy to the venture. Staying would be both wasteful and pointless. Sid Raynor, George's cousin, summed up this sad chapter in Raynor's life, years later: 'He couldn't accept the method of football in England. He felt that football here were violent.'

Raynor tried to get work in England, sending out letters to different clubs but they were not willing to take a chance on him. Raynor may well have won the Olympic Gold medal but his time at Coventry had hardly illuminated his CV. To him it appeared that this lack of response was either a reflection on his dismal failure in England, or a resolute refusal to welcome foreign ideas. The Hungarian revolution had resulted in many immigrants from the Hungarian coalmines coming to Lincolnshire, and Raynor even tried contacting the National Coal Board to see if he could physically train a group of them, but even this came to nothing: the Coal Board decided to send a physical trainer up from London to fill the role that was on

Raynor's doorstep. His time at Coventry City Football Club and the rejection by the Coal Board would remain embittering twin signposts in Raynor's life.

With no other employment on the horizon, in early 1957 he took up a job as a regional instructor and coach with the Lincolnshire Education Committee: but events were once again about to take another unexpected turn.

13

BACK TO
SWEDEN

Much had happened in Swedish football since Raynor had left in May 1954 to try his hand in Italian football. The biggest change had been the decision to permit professional footballers back into the domestic game. It is quite likely that if the World Cup had not been held in Sweden in 1958 this change might have taken a lot longer to have happened.

In Sweden in the early 1950s, all sports associations played under the aegis of the Swedish Sports' Federation, an organisation that in 1945 had imposed regulations on them forbidding professionalism in sports. It is ironic that Raynor's achievements in succeeding with amateur footballers served only to further consolidate the stance that only amateurs could be selected for the national side. It was only when the national side failed to qualify for the 1954 World Cup that the debate about using professional players in the national team gathered momentum.

The reason for that failure to qualify was widely accepted to be because the selection committee could not consider overseas players for the National XI. From January 1949, when Gunnar Nordahl became the first Swedish player to accept professional terms with Milan, until 1954 when thirty-three Swedish players had left Sweden to play in Spain, France or Italy, the Swedes had been forced to rely on their fourth-string side to try to qualify for Switzerland. In the end they lost out to a less than impressive Belgian team, relinquishing a 2-goal lead in the final match.

Accordingly, in February 1956, with an eye on the World Cup, the Swedish Football Association voted to allow the reintroduction of professional players back into the domestic game. One of the first beneficiaries was Gunnar Gren who had returned home to play for the club side OIK after his sparkling career in Italy. Even then, bizarrely, Gren had to serve out a period of grace before he was allowed back into the national side.

In an attempt to arrest the decline in fortunes following Raynor's departure, Sweden had tried two foreign coaches, but in both cases their appointments had been without success. The first coach was the old Stoke and England international Hong Ying ('Frank') Soo. Under Soo, Sweden performed fairly well against amateur opposition but got hammered when up against quality opposition: the Soviet Union put 7 past them without response in Moscow in 1954, and then Sweden collapsed like a pack of cards against the Hungarians the following year. When Russia scored a second 6–0 victory in June 1955, that was the end of Soo.

In the autumn of 1955, Josef Stroh was chosen to coach the side, but not before Kock had made a furtive plea to Raynor to return to take charge of the Swedish attempt to participate at the Melbourne Olympic Games in 1956. However, that plea came after Jesse Carver had convinced Raynor to join him at Highfield Road, so Raynor had to turn his old friend down. Accordingly, Sweden did not submit their application to participate.

Stroh's tenure was fretful and panic started to characterise the national selection as the national selection committee, conscious of the imminence of the World Cup, became fearful of an impending international humiliation. A 3–1 defeat to the Norwegians left the team in disarray. In the next game, against Denmark in October 1956, the desperation manifested itself. In an attempt to fast-track fringe players into World Cup contention the selection committee, for whatever reason, imposed the selection of six Second Division players on Stroh.

The interference didn't stop there. With time running out during the game against Denmark, Putte Kock (the then chairman of the selection committee) took the decision to send Gosta Lofgren on as a substitute without consulting Stroh first. The substitution worked: Lofgren scored to salvage a draw but Kock, invited to a meeting with the general secretary of the Swedish FA, Holger Bergerus, resigned as a result and Eric Persson took over Kock's position. At that same meeting with Bergerus, Kock impressed upon him the need to dispense with Stroh and bring Raynor back as an adviser to help coach and train the national side. As a result the two agreed that the best course of action would be to offer Raynor a contract.

The contract that was offered would take Raynor up to 30 June 1958, the day after the 1958 World Cup Final. It was Bergerus who contacted Raynor following the Danish match. Raynor wrote of this time:

> I didn't really want to go back. I had done my stint of travelling and living abroad, and I knew that if I took my old job back again I should have to travel all over Sweden to find out the real facts and check up on the present form of the players … But, when I talked the matter over with my wife we both realised that there seemed little chance of getting a job at home, so I cabled Mr Bergerus.

In a marked contrast to his reception when he first went to Sweden in 1946, the decision to bring back Raynor was supported by the Swedish press and public. Discussing the subject of Raynor's return, Swedish historian Jesper Zenk had this to say: 'The failure to qualify for the 1954 World Cup was regarded as a fiasco. In light of his previous successes, Raynor was the sole choice with international experience available prior to the home World Cup.'

By being an outsider Raynor was also immune to the constant reminders that would be likely to come his way if he'd been a Swede and were to fail – a Swedish coach who failed at home in the 1958 World Cup would never be allowed to forget it. Another plus was that Raynor had worked in Italy. The Swedish squad had several professional players plying their trade in Italian clubs, and having a coach with experience from Serie A was a massive boost in terms of international credibility.

On his return to Sweden in March 1957, Raynor convened a conference with all the league clubs and received assessments from each of them regarding the form of their current playing staff. At the conference, Bergerus announced that Raynor was to be given a free hand over training and tactics. The personnel of the selection committee might have changed, but the implicit respect for Raynor's methods and promptings remained. In Eric Persson, the Malmo President and chairman of the three-man selection committee, Raynor had a link between the national squad, the league clubs and the National Association; similarly with Eric Hallden, the ex-chairman of Norkopping and Einar Jonasson, who had been placed in charge of youth development; a key figure in the Stars of the Future courses.

As Mr Zenk went on to write:

> The Swedish squad was among the oldest ever seen at a World Cup. But Raynor was quite content to build the team around his most trusted players from 1948 – Nils Liedholm and Gunnar Gren. With Liedholm and Gren, he always knew they had maximum respect for him, and as they were the most commanding players in the squad, the players listened to him.

Raynor would have no final vote as to the selection of the team, but he was given the opportunity to advise as to team selection and believed this 'arrangement' as being the best for all concerned. For his first game against Austria in May 1957 Raynor advised against the use of any Second Division players and suggested instead that the side should be based around the domestic champions Norkopping, debuting four players from that side. Next he suggested the inclusion of the goalkeeper Svensson (Helsingborgs), the defender, Bergmark (Orebro) and Gunnar Gren (OIK). A single goal defeat to the Austrians followed – 'but we were on our way back', wrote Raynor.

With Raynor coaching the side, Sweden won the 1957 Nordic Cup, and he now strengthened the side by encouraging the selection of Sigge Parling, a tough tackling defensive player nicknamed the 'Iron Stove'. Raynor had first come across Parling in 1948 in Bosön, at one of the Stars of the Future courses, and he would go on to prove invaluable to Sweden during the World Cup. Parling remembered: 'George always had a cheerful tone. He was a good and happy person, who was superb at creating a team and ensuring that the amount of training was just right. He had a lot of England in him but he also had such an insight into football.'

Raynor now went about personally getting to know the players who he considered to be probables for the World Cup Final squad, even to the extent of staying with each international player for a number of days to get to know them and build friendships and understanding. During the 1957 Nordic Cup, Raynor had uncovered another of his famous finds, this time Agne Simonsson, a brilliant centre forward who scored a spectacular headed goal against Norway within 40 seconds of his debut. Simonsson was a wonderfully willowy player, blessed with the ability to bring the ball quickly under control. He later said, 'I came in contact with George in 1957, when I was selected for my first International. He believed in me, so I had the advantage of that, he was coach.' In the glare of publicity, Simonsson's nerves got the better of him however, and he sought out Raynor for special advice. In order not to go backwards during the close season lull going into the World Cup year, Raynor 'mapped out a pattern of circuit training, and other work that I could do indoors – or when possible, outside on the snow, wrapped up like an Eskimo! In this, I worked alone, and made sure that I kept up to the mark physically.'

Simonsson was a fan of Raynor, saying of him: 'George thought we had such a good team [for the World Cup], and it was he who composed it.' But Simonsson's arrival did not alleviate the immediate concern Raynor had of the squad's chances generally if the 'Italian brigade' were not able to be included in the final squad. Without 'the Italian brigade', Raynor knew the home-based stars would have difficulty progressing through the competition: 'That was why I was so anxious to recruit our Italian-based players for the World Cup matches. It would have been impossible for us to meet world opposition without such performers as Liedholm [and others].'

After the success of the Nordic Cup, the season was concluded by another 0–1 reverse, this time against the current World Cup holders West Germany and which hardened Raynor's conviction that to make any kind of progress in the World Cup Sweden would have to bring the best of the 'foreign' Swedish professionals back into the fold. What Raynor needed, clearly, was a general acceptance that rather than select only those players – like Gren – who had come back to Sweden to play out their careers, he could select any of those still playing overseas, such as Kurt Hamrin and Nils Liedholm. It was during the discussions with the selection committee that Raynor advised that this plan was the only way forward and so initiated the debate as to what would be best for Sweden during the World Cup.

Such was the entrenched attitude against professionalism that the biggest hurdle would be that of changing public opinion. Raynor repudiated the withering criticism he received for seeking professionals to bolster his squad by writing: 'It was claimed that the Swedish [World] Cup side was not representative of Swedish football. Perhaps it wasn't, but it was representative of the footballers Sweden produced.' As time went on, however, the Swedes welcomed the change, and it was certainly a move welcomed by the home-based players: 'We were very lucky that the professionals came over for the World Cup,' said Bengt Berndtsson. 'It was a very popular choice for them to return.'

As a result, in January 1958, Holger Bergerus went cap in hand to Italy to negotiate the release of the professionals contracted to the clubs in Serie A. His negotiating partner was the old Norkopping boss Lajos Czeizler, who had been coaching in Italy since 1949. Raynor did not want to bring in a squad of Swedish 'foreigners' en masse; his desire was to add foreign-based players to a home-grown squad and he knew exactly which ones he wanted. In this regard, Raynor purposefully selected only those who he was either familiar with or who were familiar with him and his methods.

The first was Nils Liedholm, captain of the squad, who had just won the 1958 Scudetto with Milan, and had gained a Gold medal under Raynor at the London Olympics. Second, playing for Atalanta was Bengt 'Julle' Gustavsson, the midfielder who John Charles, the famous Welsh international then playing for Juventus, said was the best centre half he had ever played against and who had been a squad member at the 1952 Helsinki Olympics.

Third on his list was Kurt Hamrin, who scored 20 goals from the right-wing that year playing for Padova. He had become familiar with George's training methods as a young player when he first started out with AIK and Raynor had famously played him against the Hungarians in November 1953.

Fourth was the left-winger Lennart 'Nacka' Skoglund, then playing at Internazionale, who had been Raynor's 'find' before the 1950 World Cup. And finally Arne Selmosson, the 27-year-old striker at Lazio who was one of the highest earners in Italian football, the 'Ray of Moonlight' who could play inside or outside right with equal skill. During the 1954/55 season he had played for Udinese and had scored home and away against Raynor's Lazio. Although a goalscorer of unquestionable credentials, Selmosson did not suit Raynor's attacking method. Raynor would stick to using a deep-lying forward to spring attacks from the midfield. Selmosson, on the other hand, revelled in bursts of acceleration and short passing, holding the ball up in the forward line. In the end he would play only 1 match in the finals and it is a measure of the clout that Raynor wielded, that his belief that Selmosson – one of the highest-paid players in the world – was not right for the balance of the team was accepted by the selection committee.

It was clear that the Italian clubs would not permit any of the professionals to depart during the Italian domestic season, which would leave just days before the 1958 World Cup competition began. The Italian clubs finally agreed to release the players, but only after securing indemnities. In *The Story of the World Cup*, Brian Glanville remarks that when Atalanta permitted Gustavsson to play in the latter stages of the World Cup, they did so only on payment by the Swedish FA of 25,000kr. Moreover, Gustavsson was held back by his employers, later writing: 'I came from Italy direct to play matches.' This highlights just how difficult it was for Raynor: the Italian League finished on 25 May 1958, and the World Cup kicked off just twelve days later, on 6 June 1958. When interviewed, Bengt Berndtsson confirmed that the full squad only congregated just before the World Cup.

Obviously this affected what tactics Raynor could ask of the team, so rather than attempt to introduce any radical initiatives he relied instead on the skills of his professional players, playing up to their strengths, which is one of the reasons why Skoglund and Hamrin achieved such prominence during the course of the competition.

In contrast, a great deal is made of the way that Brazil successfully introduced 4–2–4 at the World Cup finals that year – an initiative which had been a long time in the making. Vincente Feola, the Brazil coach, had spent years conceiving of the tactics that would underpin Brazil's attempt to win that World Cup, while in comparison Raynor had a mere twelve days to familiarise his squad with what he intended to do. The principles that Raynor had grown up with, in an environment where you made do with what you had, were now about to be put to the ultimate test.

Agne Simonsson, Sweden's young striker, remarked of Raynor's successful methods during that competition: 'There's no doubt about it. Maybe he did not evolve us tactically, but he managed to find the right players and the right way to play.' Raynor had got 'the blend right' in the team, in Skoglund and Hamrin they had the two best wingers in the competition, and in Simonsson himself, one of the best centre forwards there. Simonsson was right in that Raynor was still persisting with tactical formations that had become dated when others – notably Brazil – had moved on. However, Raynor saw the benefit in using his fast wingers to cross to late arriving forwards and there's no doubt that this was still an effective strategy.

Some England players did not think the Swedish team or the tactics they used were all that special. Johnny Haynes, in particular, announced that England would have easily beaten Sweden by stopping their wingers but when this theory of containment was put to the test (in 1959 at Wembley); it failed and Sweden ran out 3–2 winners.

The fact that can't be ignored is that until the final match in the World Cup, Sweden's opponents had struggled to contain Kurt Hamrin and Lennart Skoglund. Such attacking tactics confirmed Raynor's attitude that to succeed in football you needed to impose your tactics and not simply contain the threat from your opponents.

Sweden's principle weakness lay in their defence. When it came to the final against Brazil, who played four along the front with Garrincha picking up the ball deep and running past the left-back, Brazil had little difficulty overcoming them. Although, that being said, so strong were their wingers and forwards that their defence was rarely tested during the competition.

When the finals' draw was made in Stockholm on 8 February 1958, the hosts were drawn in Group C alongside Hungary, Mexico and Wales. The biggest threat to Sweden in the group should have come from the Hungarians. Hidegkuti, Grosics and Bozsik still remained of those who had done so well in the previous World Cup and added to them was a fantastic left-sided player in Lajos Tichy. However, they had suffered greatly after the last World Cup, losing their best players when Puskas, Czibor and Kocsis had refused to return to the country when on tour during the counter-revolution in 1956. Hungary would lose, embarrassingly, in Oslo in their first World Cup qualifying game in 1957, and when they did qualify for Sweden they would show themselves to be a sad shadow of their former selves. Whereas they had dazzled with their play and team formation in 1954, in 1958 they would now use roughhouse intimidation to characterise their involvement. Glanville quoted Sebes as later saying of the 1958 squad: 'I have never seen a Hungarian team in such a deplorable physical condition and nervous state.'

Otherwise, the group appeared to be made up of also-rans with Mexico and the British representatives Wales, who had only qualified due to a stroke of good fortune.

Wales had already been eliminated by the Czechs in a European Qualifying Group. However, when Israel's Arab opponents had all withdrawn rather than play them, FIFA decided that Israel would have to fulfil at least one game to ensure qualification. Wales were pulled out of the hat (both Uruguay and Belgium had turned down the opportunity when they were pulled first and second) and then Wales proceeded to record home and away victories against the Israelis to ensure qualification for all four British sides for the first, and so far, the only time in World Cup history.

Like most observers, Raynor's attention was drawn to John Charles, the Welsh centre half or centre forward then playing with Juventus. In a group containing Gunnar Gren, Simonsson and Jozef Bozsik, John Charles was easily the main man but the World Cup would not see the best of him.

Of the other qualifiers for the finals, there was a personal interest for Raynor in the participation of the England team. He would come to use their performance as a benchmark by which to judge the success of his own side but he still held the British in high regard. Raynor had already been in contact with Walter Winterbottom before April, offering to help him find a place to base the England team. Brian Glanville has recorded that Raynor criticised the England set-up when he allegedly said that it was a 'sin and a shame' that England based themselves in the centre of Gothenburg at the Park Avenue Hotel. However, according to Bob Ferrier, a different version of this story exists which contradicts the one that Glanville trots out.

Ferrier records the fact that Winterbottom was due to go to Sweden on 7 February 1958 in order to attend the World Cup draw on 8 February.

From Stockholm, Winterbottom's intention was to assess a shortlist of possible training venues but because of the Munich air disaster on 6 February, he delayed his trip, staying in London while news of the disaster spread. When Winterbottom finally got to Sweden, the Brazilians and Russians had already taken Hindas, 20km outside Gothenburg, which would have been his preferred venue. Lisekil, where the Austrians stayed, would otherwise have been perfect but since England were playing all their games in Gothenburg the six-hour journey for each of their three group games from that town was considered too much.

Winterbottom therefore contacted Raynor, who suggested the Park Avenue Hotel. 'It had quality, first-class service, and was quiet,' wrote Ferrier, 'and Raynor felt that Gothenburg was by no means riotous and was in many ways like an English provincial city. In fact, the hotel proved to be excellent and served good but not over-rich food; there was also some music, so that the players did not entirely feel cut off from all human ken.'

It was a popular choice with the players and was infinitely better than the Luxor Hotel where England had based themselves for the 1950 World Cup in Rio de Janeiro. Whereas out of town hotels had grounds where the players could train, this did not cause England too much of a problem either because the players could undertake training on the Gothenburg pitch.

The Swedish public had little confidence in the chances of their team, but the lead-up to the competition went relatively smoothly for Raynor's squad. He encouraged the marvellous team-spirit that characterised the Swedish effort that year and, as Bengt Berndtsson explained, Raynor maintained that spirit with simply light training on each day throughout the competition. This was one of Raynor's great fundamental strengths.

He was such a well-liked man that his optimism galvanized the team. In English League football this friendliness had placed Raynor at odds with the tough professional culture, but here in Sweden, in the days leading up to and during the 1958 World Cup finals, it served to perfectly settle the nerves. Parling remembered George's special way of rousing all the lads in the dorms each day during training camp: 'Every morning he went around and sang to wake the guys. He had a raspy voice and was as keen as a squirrel.'

Gustavsson later wrote: 'Mr Raynor's main task was to inspire and coach the team just before and during the World Cup matches. He did that with good humour and did it in his playful style. We liked him very much. He really was a big inspiration to us all!' By his own admission, Raynor knew that such frivolity wouldn't be enough for Sweden to do well in the World Cup, but neither would it benefit the team to inundate them with initiatives that had not been tried and tested, so he purposely kept pressure off the team by keeping training light, and keeping the spirit of the players up. 'George played a large part in us becoming the runners up in the World Championships,' said Parling. 'Many coaches can add too much training for a tournament, but George could really administer training properly. It is important.'

Raynor had absolute belief in the skill of the players in the squad but he also kept everyone's feet on the ground. Having made a confident boast before the competition started that Sweden would get to the final, after the game versus Hungary he said, 'Sweden are the slowest team in the competition. If there was a relay race over a hundred yards between all the different countries, Sweden would finish last.' But with his faith in the team remaining firm he added, 'But we will still reach the final.'

14

THE 1958
WORLD CUP

The Swedes opened the tournament against Mexico in front of a full house in Solna. Raynor brought in Bror Mellberg at inside right to really get in amongst the Mexican midfielders who he saw as light tacklers. Svensson was forced into a double save when the Mexicans applied early pressure, but it was Sweden who scored first, through Agne Simonsson.

Raynor had told both Skoglund and Hamrin to come 10 yards in from the touchline when the ball was on the other side of the field of play, and the benefit of this tactic worked to Sweden's advantage here. Liedholm's cross-field pass from the right found Skoglund on the left apex of the penalty area and he took his defender on, got to the goal-line and crossed into the goal area where Simonsson got ball side of his marker and placed the ball to the left side of Carbajal in the Mexico goal. In the second half, Liedholm's drive from outside the box smashed against the bar and then, minutes later, Hamrin was fouled in the area. Liedholm, typically measured and calm, put away the re-taken penalty after referee Latyshev noticed an infringement. These goals set Sweden on their way to a 3–0 victory. Later the same day no fewer than 7 further matches were played: in 1958 all the countries would play on the same day as the opening game.

Immediately on the conclusion of the game Raynor rushed to the airport for a flight to Sandviken, 125 miles to the north so that he could watch the match between Wales and Hungary. 'I tried to persuade the police to let me tuck my car in behind the King's so that I could escape quickly from the stadium,' Raynor said. 'But it was worthwhile because I picked up plenty of points [about the play of Wales and Hungary].'

When Sweden did meet Hungary four days later, Hamrin netted halfway through each half. The first came from Skoglund's cross, when once again the opposition had allowed him to get into the area. This time, he crossed into a confused mess of a defence and the ball, as if in a pinball machine, broke free to Hamrin, 10 yards out and unmarked, who put it into the net. In the second half, Hamrin, from what appeared to be an offside position, was chased down on the edge of the area, and then sent an excellent lob over Groscis into the left side of the net. Liedholm contrived to roll a penalty wide of the post later before Tichy's consolation goal whizzed past Svensson.

Sweden had qualified from their group, but it had come with a certain amount of home court advantage. Writing later, Willy Meisl declared that 'even Swedish critics thought referee Mowatt (Scotland) had made two decisions which hit the Magyars very hard. Hamrin's goal appeared offside and a harmless charge against Simonsson was penalized by a penalty.' It wouldn't be the last time a British referee messed up in a World Cup, nor would it be the last World Cup where the home side were favoured by refereeing decisions.

Raynor did not let his emotions run away with him. The win guaranteed qualification, and while his 'elderly' team may have contributed to a view that they were slow, in reality he had set them up with a deliberate pattern to play to, and this reduced their speed. A cross-field ball to the opposing winger will always result in the play being held up, but that movement across field to bring the ball into the goal area for the late arriving forward – reminiscent once again of the pre-war Bury 'school of thought' – was showing itself to be devastatingly effective.

1. Alan Crossley, uncle of Welsh international goalkeeper Mark, standing on Furnace Hills. This was once a shale-covered field where George Raynor first played for the Wesleyan Chapel in the Bible League. Now covered in long grass, maturing trees dot the field where Raynor would have slalomed his way down the wing.

2. All that remains of the King Street School, Hoyland. To the left of the picture is the area which, formerly, housed a bowling green, alongside which George would practise sprinting and running and where he first met Phyllis Whitfield as a teenager.

3. The former Wesleyan Chapel (now demolished), on Church Street, Elsecar where George first attended Thomas Tomlinson's Bible Class.

4. 25 May 1930: a photograph taken on the day George Raynor and Phyllis Whitfield married.

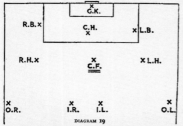

62	ASSOCIATION FOOTBALL

of filling up to some extent the large area of 'no-man's-land' in the W-formation. It has the additional advantage of having four forwards constantly on the attack, prompted, in effect, by three halves—for the defensive centre-forward really becomes an extra centre half-back. The two inside forwards move a little

nearer towards each other, so that the simple formation shown in Diagram 19 results. The underlying fault of this formation is that the three lines which compose it are all parallel with the goal-lines. An improved variation, provided the necessary players are forthcoming, is to have two centre-forwards. This has been tried with success by certain professional clubs, notably Luton Town. One inside-forward adopts the role of attacking centre-half, and it improves the scheme if the wing-halves mark the opposing outsides

ATTACK	63

and the full-backs the insides. This gives great thrust down the full length of the middle of the field, as will be seen from Diagram 20.

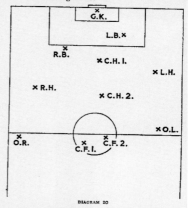

The last attacking formation to be discussed is one which I have purposely left until the end, and that is the 'lop-sided W-formation.' In case this phrase conveys nothing to the reader, the method of attack is

6. An extract from F.N.S. Creek's *Association Football* published in 1937 which evidenced the commonality of a withdrawn centre forward in the English game prior to the Second World War. This was the method favoured by Norman Bullock at Bury where Ernie Matthews was the 'G-man' centre forward. Reference to Luton Town in 1937 was apt; they won the Third Division (South) that season.

7. Highbury, 1947: Gunnar Nordahl, demonstrating the balance and positioning which made him such a threat as an attacker, scores for Sweden past England's Frank Swift. This was the game in which Raynor reverted back to the method first used by Norman Bullock at Bury in the 1920s and used Nordahl as a deep-lying centre forward but which really amounted to him being an attacking roving midfielder who dictated play. This position (which Raynor dubbed 'the G-man') was later used by Nandor Hidegkuti, was copied by Ronnie Allen, Don Revie and popularised by Johann Cruyff who is the principle reason for Spain's current success; and consequently the current success of Bayern Munich.

FOOTBALL ASSOCIATION OF IRELAND

OFFICIAL PROGRAMME

International Match

World's (Jules Rimet) Cup

IRELAND

v.

SWEDEN

SUNDAY, NOVEMBER 13, 1949

AT

DALYMOUNT PARK, DUBLIN

KICK-OFF   2.30 p.m.

Secretary

6D..

8. November 1949: the programme for the World Cup qualifier between Ireland and Sweden played in Dublin. This was the game in which Kalle Palmer belied his weak appearance and scored a hat-trick to secure Sweden's qualification to Brazil. Arguably, Raynor's finest achievement for victory was achieved against quality opposition and despite the loss of the majority of the 1948 Olympic Gold medal side.

9. November 1949: A desperate lunge by Torsten Lindberg in the Swedish penalty area helps avert an Irish indirect free-kick awarded in Sweden's area during the World Cup qualifier in Dublin. Hasse Jeppson, later of Charlton Athletic, stands at the end of the Swedish wall.

10. November 1953: A clear indication as to the deep-lying role that Harry Johnston adopted against the Hungarians. In the picture Johnston (white No. 5) is to be found inside the goal area for Hungary's second goal. Note otherwise the England formation: Matthews (No. 7) is standing far away on the right-wing, undertaking no defensive duties.

11. November 1953: Instead of seeking to go and mark Hidegkuti (as mistakenly shown here in Marshall Cavendish's *Book of Football* around 1971) Harry Johnston, the Blackpool centre half, deliberately stayed back in defence during the game: a decision which was inspired by a tactical talk given by George Raynor to Walter Winterbottom in the days before the game.

12. Around 1956: A dynamic shot of one of the great unfulfilled talents of British football: Alick Jeffrey. A mercurial striker, prodigious from a young age, Jeffrey's career was effectively ended by injury in 1956 and then, incredibly, resurrected by a course of training and coaching devised for him by George Raynor when manager of Skegness Town of the Midland League in 1959.

For the final game of the group, against Wales, Raynor dropped his 'first' team and asked the selection committee to allow the reserves in the squad to play in the game. It was a clever decision on the part of Raynor. Not only did it blood those squad players who might not otherwise stand a chance of playing in the finals, but it also offered them all a genuine chance to impress the coach enough to be considered for the first team. The major beneficiary of this was Reino Borjesson, who did so well against Wales at left-back that Liedholm was moved from right half to inside left against the Russians: Borjesson then stayed in the side up until and into the final. Bengt Berndtsson, who played in the game versus Wales, explained: 'George didn't give us special instructions before the game. He just told us to play our normal game. Us reserves accepted that we were in to give the first XI a rest.'

This, in retrospect, was the big moment for Wales; for their country and their football. This was their opportunity to impose themselves on a World Cup lacking a clear favourite but an absence of (national?) self-confidence would be their undoing and they would pay dearly for not going for the win.

Given that Sweden had already qualified and Raynor had brought in the reserves, one is almost tempted to conclude that he was purposely offering Wales a chance to automatically qualify. If that was his intention, no one told Jimmy Murphy, the Wales coach. 'Wales could and should have won,' Raynor said, 'but their tactics were based on the safety-first principle … it seemed Wales went into the match determined not to lose.'

Raynor was particularly scathing of the decision to restrain the match-winning ability of big John Charles, positioned as a centre half when (in Terry Medwin's absence) the Welsh forward line clearly needed his talent to unlock the Swedish defence. What is more, the Welsh were so negative that they invited the Swedes to attack them. On another day Skoglund would have put away any number of the chances that he missed. In the end the two sides cancelled each other out, and Charles, for one, wrote that he was embarrassed by the fact that the crowd had paid to watch such a game.

By drawing o–o instead of winning the game Wales had now to play-off with Hungary for a spot in the quarter-finals.

A brutal game followed.

'It was one of the roughest and worst games of the tournament,' wrote Meisl. 'The Russian referee, Latyshev, let many blatant fouls pass, especially several rugby tackles against giant John Charles, who – slightly injured and obviously careful – never reached anything like his true form in Sweden.' Kicked all game by Sipos, and unprotected by a referee strangely indulgent of such play by his Eastern bloc neighbours, John Charles was unable to play against Brazil, who would ultimately only beat Wales by the merest of margins, thus fueling an 'if only' debate amongst the Welsh.

Sweden were now drawn against Russia in the quarter-finals. The Russians had, like Wales, also survived a play-off match, albeit a much less violent game against England, and would also pay for having to participate in it with their tiredness. The play-offs took place on the evening of the 17th June 1958, with the quarter-finals scheduled for the afternoon of the 19th June. Tellingly, none of the three nations who qualified via the play-offs would win their quarter-final. Certainly, the benefit of this scheduling to Raynor was immense because it allowed him to watch the England v Russia game, flying from Stockholm to Gothenburg.

Raynor noted that the key feature in the game was the way Yuri Voinov had contained Johnny Haynes. Raynor observed that Voinov would disrupt English attacks by intercepting passes to Haynes, or, when Haynes was in possession, would keep tight and pressure him toward the left-hand side of the centre line. That being done, the Russian right midfield and defence would mark the English left-wingers and intercept any diagonal cross-field balls that Haynes could otherwise supply.

For the Russian game, Raynor brought Liedholm back into the forward line at inside left and gave him specific instructions to do unto Voinov what Voinov had done to Haynes, but with a slight twist: to closely mark him when the Russians were in possession or, if Voinov was marking Liedholm, for Liedholm to move upfield into the Russian area and take Voinov with him. The effect of this was that when Russia counter-attacked, Voinov would be so far down field as to be useless to the attack.

Sweden scored first through Hamrin. The goal was a fortunate one. He ran unchallenged into the area, his side pass bounced off Kaserev and Hamrin, continuing his run, opportunistically headed the ball past the wrong-footed Yashin. Hamrin later said:

> Against Russia I had been on the losing side first in Moscow [Sweden losing 7–0] and then losing 6–0 at the Rasunda. [As a result] we didn't have much confidence before the [quarter-final]. Even a player such as Orvar Bergmark [the Swedish right back that day] had packed his bags to go home, thinking the tournament was over for us. But, luckily, something else happened. Personally I think this was Sweden's best game in the entire tournament, I scored a goal and assisted on the other goal that Simonsson scored.

Hamrin's cross for Simonsson was exquisite. Chasing down a ball heading out of play, he cut it back from the byline and there was Simonsson, unmarked, to finish the job – yet another goal from Gigg Lane! When interviewed after the game against Russia, Raynor stated that he had felt that Sweden would have beaten the Russians 'in any circumstances': but the drain of having to play the play-off had definitely assisted the Swedes.

What came next was a splendidly controversial semi-final against the World Champions, West Germany. Brian Glanville makes a big play of the change in national mood, with the excesses of nationalism manifesting themselves in the pre-match machinations of the game. 'The match,' he wrote, 'provided an extraordinary study in national behaviour, as the Swedes' unfettered chauvinism put even the Germans' in the shade, and very nearly resulted in the game not being played at all.'

The legacy of the game would leave a bitter taste in the mouth but there was also controversy in the lead up to the game.

The German press in Berlin and Hamburg had run a campaign in the early stages of the competition criticising Swedish food and the cost of living. Sepp Herberger, the German coach, had assumed that the Argentinians would win their section and therefore concluded that their semi-final would be played in Stockholm. As it happened, West Germany won Group A and now found themselves in Gothenburg where Helmut Schoen, at short notice, had to find a hotel with enough rooms to accommodate the squad. After asking the Swedish organising committee to assist, the only hotel available was the Gottskars-Kur Hotel, which was not popular amongst the players. As a result, the players spoke to the press about the hotel, and the press interpreted this as a deliberate ploy by the Swedes to unbalance the Germans.

Further problems were encountered by the ticketing. Trusting Herberger's intended course through the competition, the German FA had overbooked on the tickets for the Stockholm semi-final and – purely as a contingency – had reserved only 1,000 tickets for Gothenburg. When the German press realised only 1,000 tickets would be available for Germans in Gothenburg it was used by the Hamburg press as yet more evidence of an attempt to upset the Germans.

Further fanning the flames of German paranoia was a terrifically successful press campaign by the *Bild* newspaper, who increased their issues by half a million copies during the competition. An unsightly kerfuffle blew up in the hour before the game when Dr Paco Bauwens (the head of the German Football Association) demanded that rows of seats be made available to the Germans. The Swedes relented and dozens of Swedish supporters had to find alternative places in the stadium to accommodate the German supporters.

The match got underway in front of a packed house. Hamrin later commented:

> I had never played an international against [West Germany] but since they had won the previous World Cup they were the big favourites.

> So we [would] play as the underdogs again, which has always been
> Sweden's best approach to a game. If I could have an opinion, I'd have
> to say that Germany was the best team – but playing at home, the crowd
> and everything else lifts your ability just a little bit more …

Raynor decided to keep to his plan of playing Liedholm 'once again in the general's role of inside left' but now asked him to play differently to the way he had against Russia. Now Liedholm would hold the ball, drawing the Germans into the middle of the field and giving the wingers greater space to operate out on the wings.

Sweden started wastefully, as many as a dozen fine chances were missed by the Swedes in the opening half. After 25 minutes, Seeler, chasing down a ball racing out of play, crossed diagonally back for Hans Schaefer, unmarked on the left-hand side of the area, to put the Germans ahead with a bullet volley past Svensson. Seeler then missed a glorious chance to put the game to bed when fed by Fritz Walter from the right; but just after the half-hour mark, a purposeful move down the centre of the park saw Gren feed Skoglund, who raced his shot from the left past Herkenrath's reach and into the right-hand corner. The match was still finely balanced when, just on the hour mark, Hamrin got into a tussle with Juskowiak. Film of the incident indicates that Juskowiak was unlucky to be sent off. Hamrin can be seen playing a ball too far in front of him on the left-hand side of the field, and Juskowiak forcefully playing the ball back down the park in front of the on-rushing Swede: the camera moves aside and, in the periphery, Hamrin goes down. Hamrin then gets up and pushes the German. Mayhem. Juskowiak protested for minutes, angrily pushing Fritz Walter and Hans Schafer away as they tried to escort him off the field. Of the incident, Hamrin recalled: 'I have to say that the knock he gave me when he got sent off wasn't that bad, but he had made a lot of unfair tackles so I imagine he had made a real collection of what today would have been yellow cards and had certainly been responsible for more than two that day.'

The Germans didn't give up. Cieslarczyk dropped back into defence and for the next 15 minutes Germany kept up the pressure. Two clear chances were sent over the bar. Their attacking movement and passing was precise and dangerous. There was still time for Parling to go strongly into the tackle with Fritz Walter, a foul that was occasioned with no sanction from the referee. The significance of the challenge was clear. Walter was so badly injured by the tackle as to be of no further use to the Germans thereafter. Raynor's desire to instil an iron edge into the pleasantries of Swedish football had achieved an arguably successful goal. It was that tackle rather than Juskowiak's sending off that turned the game, because Walter was the architect of the German's attack, and the Germans were still causing the Swedish defence numerous problems through the centre of the field.

With 10 minutes to go, Sweden hammered home the final nail in the German coffin. From a breakaway, Skoglund passed to Hamrin, whose shot was parried by Harkenrath: the ball reached the outside of the German area, where Gren struck a rising shot beyond Herkenrath into the top left-hand corner. Then, with moments to go, Hamrin brought the house down with an impetuous move. On the far-right side of the field, and at walking pace, he picked up the ball and beat Cieszarczk (who nudged him), Erhardt (who tried to slide tackle him on the goal-line) and Szymaniak, who had come over to cover from the front of the area, before chipping the ball impudently over Erkenrath's left shoulder at the near left post.

'My own goal [to make the score 3–1] just happened,' said Hamrin, 'just one of those things when you're in a tight spot and have decided to just hold on to the ball. It turned out the way it did. To be perfectly honest I wouldn't have a clue how it went down if I hadn't seen it on TV afterwards. It was an amazing experience.'

The fall-out from the game was immediately felt by Swedish holidaymakers in the summer months following the competition.

Whilst in Germany, some reported that their car tyres had been slashed, the locals having noted the Swedish licence plates and targeted them. The legacy on the Continent would be longer lasting. Even as late as 1961, in the play-off against Switzerland in Berlin for the final place in Chile, the Swedes and Raynor would experience great hostility.

Sweden had not been expected to get to the final. 'Nobody had fancied us,' wrote Raynor, 'and the British Press just about ignored us. Only one writer – Kenneth Wolstenholme, the BBC television commentator writing in the *Sunday Graphic* – had given us a ghost of a chance.' It was, Hamrin later said, a mood that had communicated itself to the players:

> There was no discussion before the game about how we should play. We were just to go in and continue what we had started. We already had the training camp, the preparatory games, the follow up throughout the tournament. In reality we had nothing to lose, we'd already done more than anyone had expected. That we then scored the first goal was something that just happened. Sure, we players did talk about that the rain could be an advantage for us. The Brazilians weren't used to it, that was what we thought, but they were just as good on a wet pitch. So no excuses there.

In his book *World Cup 1958*, John Campkin observed that during the final, Sweden tried to mark Didi zonally as opposed to man-to-man, as England and Wales had both done. Raynor felt, however, that the way to deal with Didi was to share the responsibility between the inside forward (Liedholm) and a wing half-back (Parling). By doing so he was not sacrificing a player to the Brazilians as the English were content to do in their group fixture. As Campkin wrote of the final: 'The inevitable result was that Didi, operating skilfully in the territory between the two, escaped challenge from either until he had drawn Sweden's defence out of position and flicked a pass away to a colleague.'

England and Wales might have stopped or slowed Brazil's attack (drawing 0–0 in the group and losing 0–1 in the quarter-finals respectively) but they had not scored against Brazil and you can't win a World Cup by not scoring. Raynor's theory of containment echoed the way he had coached the side in 1953 to play defensively while still allowing for counter-attacks against the Hungarians. That had opened the game up for the Swedes to attack the defence.

The problem for Sweden in the final was that not only were the Brazilians better players, but by playing 4–2–4 Brazil had numerical advantage against the Swedish defence – if Parling was marking Didi, then Gustavsson would have to fall back to mark Pele and therefore neglect his attacking duties. In addition, the Brazilians were not all about attack. Their side was built on a solid defence with a good back four and the two midfielders and Zagallo ready to drop back to help out. This made inevitable the result and it is notable that none of the Swedish players interviewed for this book felt that Sweden could have won the final.

Raynor decided to keep his side for the final. His famous phrase that Brazil would 'panic all over the show' if Sweden scored first finds no place in his book. Instead Raynor writes of his utter satisfaction in having taken Sweden as far as he possibly could have taken them.

The 1958 Brazilian World Cup Final side was one of the twentieth century's great footballing sides: 'Not one football team in the world could have beaten the Brazil of that day.'

In the lead up to the final the Brazilians had decided to drop de Sordi and instead play Djalma Santos in his place at right-back, a move designed specifically to neutralise Skoglund's influence down the left-wing. In the semi-final, the French winger, Roger Piantoni had caused de Sordi a few problems and it was felt that Djalma Santos would cope better with the threat presented by Skoglund's pace. Nilton Santos, meanwhile, would take care of Hamrin on the right-wing, while in the middle Orlando and the captain, Bellini, would cope with Simonsson and the two inside forwards, Liedholm and Gren. Of the 'two' Brazilian midfielders (4–2–4 was arguably 4–3–3 since Zagallo was used in a deep-lying inside role), Zito would be used in a holding role as the right half but Didi, the incredible left half, would provide much of the attacking impetus with his vision and promptings. Indeed, Didi and Garrincha were the key characters in the line-up.

Brazil's forward line was excellent.

On the right-wing was Garrincha, who would fly past Sven Axbom twice in the first 10 minutes to produce the first 2 goals. One of the best wingers in the history of the game, Garrincha could be unstoppable and win matches single-handedly with his verve and athleticism as England were to find out in the quarter-finals of the World Cup in 1962.

In the centre was Vava (let's call him 'a conventional centre forward'). Playing a little behind Vava at inside left was Pele – only 17 years of age but already making his mark on the competition. He was strong in possession and displayed a speed of thought that enabled him to overcome what appeared insurmountable obstacles. In the quarter-final his snap shot had wrong-footed Jack Kelsey and defeated the gallant Welsh side.

On the left of the forward-line was Mario Zagallo. Zagallo was not a conventional winger, but he showed his appetite to fight and run throughout the game, tracking back to assist Didi when Sweden were in possession.

If there was a lacuna then it was down the left side, because a counter-attack ball played into the hole, wide right of the Brazilian defence, would have caused some hesitancy on the part of Nilton Santos, and would fall into the vacant space to the left of Didi.

There may have been no discussion before the game as to how Raynor wanted Sweden to specifically play against Brazil but the general idea was to continue in the same vein that they had approached each match in the tournament. So far Sweden had been at their best when attacking opponents and so it remained the plan here. This could not be done if the instruction was simply to man mark Didi because the Swedes would fall back into their defensive third and invite trouble. After all, Didi may have positioned himself as a left half but he was, putatively, an inside left so his natural game was to attack when in possession.

Raynor prayed for two things and got them both. The first thing was for rain – all night and into the Sunday morning the rain fell on the red roofs of Stockholm. The second thing was an early goal. Brazil had yet to go behind in the competition, and if this happened, he hoped that the Brazilian temperament would put paid to their composure.

The early Swedish goal was perfect. In the 4th minute Bergmark played the ball to Borjesson in the right-half position who thumped a pass into the gap behind Zagallo but in front of Nilton Santos. Simonsson, the furthest forward, had tracked over to the right-wing and struggled at first to get the ball under control. When he did, he played a straight cross over to Liedholm, again in front of the defensive four. Liedholm would perhaps have welcomed a ball on the grass, but had to control it instead with his right thigh before wrong-footing Zito and shooting under Bellini's outstretched foot to beat Gilmar's dive to the right.

However, Brazil did not panic when the goal was scored. They were quickly calling for the ball to be returned to the centre. Two goals by Vava put the Brazilians up by the quarter-hour mark. Garrincha, on the right-wing twice went past Axbom and flashed crosses across the goal area to set up both goals, tidily put away by Vava. Film of the game reveals a match played beautifully and skilfully, if at a more sedate pace than we are used to nowadays. In those days, of course, craftsmen considered their art, and workers took pride in their work. That being said, Garrincha comes across as being an utterly dangerous opponent; that burst of speed making sliding tackles appear static. Even now, considering ways of stopping him would occupy modern coaches for some time because he was fast, had excellent ball control and could go past players inside or outside.

Ten minutes after the break, Pele scored a goal alien to that time; one which belonged to the modern, faster age, and yet one that was nevertheless balletic in its execution. Beating his man to Nilton Santos' high diagonal ball into the area by chesting the ball forward, Pele allowed it to bounce, chipped it over Gustavsson's outstretched leg as the defender came forward to intercept and then, before the ball had time to land, hammered the shot past Svensson with a trampoline-like volley: 'It was an incredibly beautiful goal, a lift like that over Gustavsson and then to take the shot on the volley … You saw right there what that 17 year old would become …' said Hamrin. Brazil would go on to win 5–2.

'Excuses?' wrote Raynor. 'Of course not. The only excuse there can be for Sweden's … defeat is that Brazil had the better individual footballers and consequently the classier teamwork. In short Brazil were the masters in a glorious match played in the finest spirit in a great sporting land.'

15

HOME
AT LAST

In July 1958 George Raynor, the son of a Hoyland mine worker, became the recipient of a knighthood bestowed by the Swedish king, Gustaf VI. Of the knighthood, Raynor said it was 'one of my proudest moments'. Afterwards he returned to England and the bungalow in Winthorpe near Skegness that he had bought in October 1956 when his job at Coventry City was coming to an end. So began a curious period in Raynor's life. In the next few years he would find employment in the stores at the Skegness Butlins holiday park, would work as a sports teacher at the local school, and manage and coach Skegness Town in the Midland League.

The main reason behind his decision to return was so that his youngest son David could receive an education in England: but there was an additional motive for settling in Skegness, in that it was a place where Raynor felt very much at home and at peace. The Dunes was a lovely bungalow with a view across the North Sea. It was a secure sign that the miner's son from Hoyland had 'made it'. One of the youngsters living on Kings Avenue, John Fennell, remembered: 'George, from memory, appeared to be well-off. For one thing he had a car: the only one in the neighbourhood. We lived on Kings Avenue nearby but whereas

I was one of eight children in a three bed bungalow, George was over there on Kings Avenue, in his three bed looking onto the sea, with only a small family.'

The common conception of writers reviewing this stage of Raynor's life is that English football 'turned its back' on him: it is stated that he was 'forced' to take the manager's job at Skegness Town because no Football League club was interested in employing him. It has also been stated that he was 'reduced' to working at Butlins Holiday Camp, that he was angry and as a result wrote *Football Ambassador at Large*.

These insinuations are not true. Judging by interviews given to the local press, George appears to have been quite happy living and working in Skegness at that time. He received offers of work in football after returning to England. There were none, however, that provided enough incentive to prise him away from the retired miner's idyll in which he was now living, and I get the distinct impression that there was, at that time, only one job which could have coaxed him away from the area, that being the England managerial post.

The *Skegness Standard* was the first to interview him at The Dunes, at the end of July 1958, and when the reporter quizzed him about his future options, Raynor stated: 'I am still looking for a job but there is nothing settled yet.' His presence in Winthorpe, a suburb of Skegness, soon came to the attention of haulage contractor and town councillor Harold Swift. Swift was the chairman of Skegness Town, which had just won the Central Alliance League in 1958, and now he and his club secretary, local landowner Geoff Cooke, decided to make a real go of pushing the club forwards in the Midland League with a view to establishing football in the town.

In the 1950s the Midland League was still highly competitive and its clubs would regularly sign ex-Football League players. This was similarly true of Skegness Town, and Swift and Cooke decided that significant investment would be needed if the club was to be a contender. In early June 1958 it was announced that five players had been signed to play for Skegness the following season: Jimmy Bloomer from Wisbech, Derby County goalkeeper Terry Webster, Pat Groome from Notts County, Malcolm Tucker from Grimsby Town and Roy Brown from Doncaster Rovers. The following month Geoff Hazledine, from Southport, and George Hutchinson, from Halifax, were added to the squad and Swift secured the clubs' home ground when he obtained the freehold on Burgh Road.

It wasn't long before Raynor was also linked with the club, but the newspaper reporter covering the matter was realistic enough to accept that if a league club came calling, then he would plump for that. The reporter's view was that Raynor would most likely take up the manager's job at Peterborough since George Swindin's contract had come to an end following the 1957/58 season. Whether the post of Peterborough boss would have been sufficient to inspire Raynor is a moot point as the club never came calling, so Harold Swift decided to make good his interest and in late August 1958 had a two-hour chat with him, the outcome of which was that, on 27 August, George signed a contract making him manager of Skegness Town at £10 a week.

When interviewed following the meeting with Raynor, one of the Skegness club officials said, 'We can just [about] afford [Raynor], but we can't afford not to have him.' The next day, Raynor drove over to the ground. One of the youngsters hanging around at the club at the time, Mick French, had a vantage point on the surrealism of Raynor's arrival at the club: 'He got out of his flash Saab, a little fella in a bobble hat. He had on blue tracksuit bottoms and a yellow top with SVERIGE written across the back. We all knew … what he had achieved. It was brilliant but we couldn't quite understand how he ended up [here].'

I am half-minded to view the appointment as Skegness Town manager as one which, despite a comparatively low salary, was one which Raynor felt to be ideal. Here was a small town football club with a World Cup finalist as their new coach. Possibly in awe of what he had achieved, initial discussions allowed Raynor to believe that the club would not stand in his way of developing the team, which meant not only developing the way they played but imposing his own particular blueprint on how the club should develop and grow. If his dream had always been to achieve in England that which he had accomplished so brilliantly in Sweden then here was the opportunity to do so, because Swift gave him as much support as possible.

One of his beliefs was that a coach could take any footballer from any level and develop that player so that he could reach the highest levels. Following his experiences in Sweden, Raynor believed – and had seen the success of such a strategy – in community-wide initiatives co-ordinated so that all young players would receive the same basic training rather than being coached by different coaches in different ways. At Skegness he wanted to show that with training and perseverance, even the local youngsters, as opposed to ex-Football League professionals, could reach first-team status. Within weeks of his appointment Raynor's mind was therefore already on the future of football in Skegness, and he told the *Standard* that it was his plan that local players would form the basis of the Midland League team within a few years. With Swift's financial backing, Raynor announced that he wanted to open an evening football school for local schoolboys and youths at the local Cooperative School.

Raynor's idea was to marry a physical education course at the local grammar school with lectures and discussions about the game, saying:

> You can't make footballers but you can give them a sound basic training. Football is such a big business these days that I see no reason why we shouldn't have night schools for it. Of course, this doesn't want to be a one man show [Rex Musson, a local football coach, and Terry Webster the ex-Derby 'keeper would both help Raynor get this idea off the ground]. This is an entirely new idea in this country but I have already been successful in Stockholm. Out of a class of 23 one player [Kurt Hamrin] who had been with me since 14 years old made the full international side at outside right and nine others are now playing first division football.

By April of the following year, not only would the Skegness Town juniors club (made up entirely of the pupils from the night school) have played their first game but so too would Raynor be instituting the gold, silver and bronze scheme that had been so favoured in Sweden during what was called a 'propaganda month for youth football' in Skegness. It was during a competition that month that 13-year-old Mick French would beat Alick Jeffrey, a future England Under-23 representative player, in a keepy-uppy competition.

Raynor's first game in charge of the first team (the second match of the 1958/59 season) gave him a real insight not only into the realities of non-league football but also into the type of challenges that he would need to overcome. For their first match the players had to leave at 5.30 in the morning, make two changes on the train, and wolf down a meal en route as there was no buffet car, before jumping on board a coach for a 45-minute bus ride. Three players (Tucker, Johnston and Brown) were all out injured for the match against Ashington. Raynor reverted to his tactical use of the G-man for the game, with George Hutchinson, one of the Skegness forwards, taking on this role. However, Hutchinson kept wandering up-field during the first half and not tracking back to receive passes from the half-back line. As a result, possession was being given away in typical non-league style, with the defenders mindlessly giving the ball back to the opposition by kicking it anywhere as long as it ended up far away from the person kicking it.

Ashington made full use of the possession and won 7–0.

The crowds at Burgh Road would also be an eye-opener for Raynor. A crowd of 1,750 turned up to see the home defeat to Grantham, but the *Standard*'s reporter was particularly incensed when only 831 turned up to see the cup win over Bourne, which led him to question whether Skegness deserved to have a team in the first place!

Within weeks Raynor was instilling a more skilled ethos into the attacks. Against Denaby United the forwards displayed far greater coordination and the whole team was faster and more

accurate in their shooting than their opponents, resulting in a
5–1 victory. Although Skegness went out early in the FA Cup,
their league fortunes continued to improve as Raynor sought to
impose tactical know-how into the team's play. In beating Blyth
Spartans the *Standard*'s reporter wrote: 'In attack Skegness did
the simple thing quickly. They cut out all the elaboration and
concentrated on getting the ball to the man in the best position
by the quickest possible route.'

Raynor considered no aspect of the job beneath him
and gladly went off to the Lincoln Claytons' ground in early
December 1958 to see the reserves lose 3–1.

Just imagine, the coach who had got his side to a World Cup
Final that summer, now, in December, standing alongside
just twelve other spectators! But such were the duties of a
non-league coach.

By the end of the season, Skegness Town might have finished
27 points behind the champions Peterborough reserves but
Raynor, accepting that the club was heading forward, was more
than happy with their sixth-place finish.

During the spring of 1959, George's eldest son Brian, who had
been working as the manager of a textile company in Sweden,
now returned to live in Skegness as well, with his Swedish wife and
two young sons. A qualified football coach himself, Brian Raynor
would appear for both Skegness Town reserves and the first team
over the next couple of years. He found a job teaching English
at Eastlands, the local grammar school, not far from Winthorpe
which would later also play a role in Raynor senior's life.

16

THE MOST IMPORTANT BOOK IN ENGLISH FOOTBALL HISTORY

In March 1959 Raynor received a phone call from Alick Jeffrey. As a player Alick Jeffrey was as talented as he was unlucky. A child protégé, he had made his Football League debut for Doncaster Rovers at the age of 15 but in October 1956, when his career appeared set, he broke his leg in a representative match against France.

When Raynor first met him the young player's career was at risk of being over. Jeffrey had not played in any form of football since breaking his leg; the treatment of his injury had been so poorly managed that he was now constantly limping because the broken leg had set shorter than the other. He was overweight and there had been a prolonged delay before the insurers had paid out on the injury: and when they did, it was on the understanding that Jeffrey would never play competitive football again. Eventually Doncaster received £15,000 and Jeffrey the sum of £4,000.

Jeffrey drifted along, his career apparently in limbo, but something about the plight of the ultra-gifted player appealed to Raynor, who considered him one of the great talents in the game and proposed a 'training course' to get him back to fitness and back into the game. Was there a reflection, perhaps, of Raynor's own old injury playing a part in this?

Jeffrey recalled: 'I'd read about George Raynor taking Sweden to the World Cup final … He said to me he could do something for me and I'd nothing to lose.' So, throughout the summer of 1959, Raynor persevered in getting Jeffrey back to match fitness in time for Skegness' 1959/60 season. True to his word, he had Jeffrey ready for a pre-season game, with the fear that the club would be liable for the payment of £4,000 to the FA if they played Jeffrey allayed because it was only a friendly.

George Crawford, a youth goalkeeper at Skegness Town at that time, remembered:

> Alick Jeffrey had broken his leg and came back to Skegness to start the climb back to the professional game. He had put on a lot of weight by the time he came to us. He was 14 or 15st when he came to us. But he was a brilliant player, spraying passes all over the place, just like Johnny Haynes. He was an excellent footballer. But in one of the training games, I think it was an 8-a-side match, we had a Hungarian goalkeeper and there was a through ball and Jeffrey (who in 20 minutes had already scored a hat-trick) and the goalkeeper clashed and Jeffrey broke his leg again.

Raynor didn't give up; the leg was a setback but the coach coaxed his player back once it mended. By March 1960 Jeffrey would star in a reserve game for Skegness Town against Horden Colliery, further testament to Raynor's indomitable self-belief in his abilities to successfully coach lost causes. Raynor was forever a believer in the talent of Alick Jeffrey, saying, 'He could be compared with the best. He would certainly have been a full international but for his accidents. He was never a great one for running about, but then great players in his position are not great at running about. They can just put a foot on the ball and clap it into the net.'

Arriving at Skegness Town at the same time as Alick Jeffrey was Charlie Williams, who had been Doncaster Rover's centre half during the late 1950s and was now coming to the end of his career. The two talents, Jeffrey and Williams, had already struck up a memorable duo act on the local cabaret circuit when they had played for Doncaster Rovers. Jeffrey taught himself to play the guitar during his recuperation and with Williams singing the two played to audiences at the nightspots of the north-east. Williams found Skegness the perfect environment in order to maintain his enjoyment of the game and now, reunited with Jeffrey, the two would renew their off-field association in the clubs and pubs.

It was at this time that Williams noticed that the banter during the songs was more warmly received than the songs themselves and so began his successful career as a comedian. As for Jeffrey, despite his talent, he never did become the national hero that Raynor and Peter Doherty, his former manager at Doncaster Rovers, amongst others, expected him to become. In January 1961, still in the financial bind with the FA and unable to find a club with which to get back into professional football, Jeffrey announced that he would leave the country and play in New South Wales for the Prague club. It was cited as the real reason as to why Jeffrey never made it to big time football. When Jeffrey did come back to England – ironically playing for Doncaster Rovers under Raynor in 1968 – his chance of gaining the fame his talent deserved had gone for good.

The 1959/60 season began with the injury to Jeffrey and in August included an incident when 52-year-old George Raynor played for the first team when some of the named players turned up late for the first-team home game against Bourne. He seemed to do well according to the press report of the match, and enjoyed the experience nevertheless, turning in a competent performance on the right-wing for the club. Then in the autumn, he received a request from the Swedish Football Association to write a report on England's performance during the Home International at Ninian Park between Wales and England. Sweden were due to play England for their first ever international engagement at Wembley in October, and Raynor was asked to assess England's performance in the Autumn international. In hindsight, this request appears to have been a cover for an opportunity to bring Raynor back to Sweden.

One matter Raynor would have noted in his report was the display in Cardiff of the England goalkeeper, Eddie Hopkinson.

In the last few minutes he had failed to come for a deep cross by Cliff Jones and Graham Moore (18 years old and on debut) had headed the equaliser for Wales. This frailty was noted and it is of interest that two Swedish goals came from crosses that Hopkinson failed to deal with. 'Hopkinson,' wrote the *Playfair* reporter, 'raised queries by his failures to get to the high ones. He had the unusual and upsetting experience of being barracked by some of the spectators.' It would be his last appearance for England.

Raynor met the Swedish delegation the day before the Wembley fixture to give the Swedish manager Einar Jonasson his match report. Jonasson was accompanied on the trip by Torsten Lindberg, the 1948 Gold-medallist goalkeeper and now the Association's general secretary, and Raynor's old friend Holger Bergerus.

For the match at Wembley the Swedes, though retaining the nucleus of their World Cup Final side, had started to gather a new young team in preparation for the attempt to qualify for the 1962 World Cup finals in Chile. Geoffrey Green's report during the days leading up to the game reflected the increasing insularity felt by people in 1950s Britain. Green wrote that 'if a private Swedish whisper is to be heeded [Simonsson] is now one of the outstanding centre forwards in Europe.' That lack of insight was a far cry from the enlightenment of Green's immediate post-war reports. In comparison with the state of affairs in 1945, Britain and British football in 1959 had gone backwards, with defeat on the football field and a loss of Empire inhibiting interest beyond British shores.

The day before the game, while the Swedish selector Eric Persson walked reverently over the Wembley turf, the Swedes trained at Fulham in a reserve match and later that evening paid a social visit to the London Casino nightspot, courtesy of the Football Association. Raynor was included as their honoured guest, and it was during that evening that Bergerus pulled him to one side and asked if he would like to work for half the year in Sweden and half in the UK in order to help Sweden mount a challenge for the next World Cup.

In the game against Sweden, England's control of the game was wrestled away during a 25-minute spell as Sweden stole the match from them with 3 goals on the counter-attack to become only the second foreign side after Hungary to win at Wembley. Simonsson's 5-minute brace of goals was the main difference between the sides. He scored the first with a header after a cross from the right-wing and the second was a wonderful, curling shot from the left-hand side of the area, the attack having developed through the centre of the field. Johnny Haynes' comment that England could easily have stopped Sweden in the World Cup the previous year by stopping their wingers was now exposed for the folly it was, because on the wings Sweden had players who were better at controlling, passing and using the ball than the English.

It was an embarrassing defeat and, as with the fall-out following the defeat by Hungary in 1953, there would be notable casualties, not least Brian Clough. This was the last time he would play for England. He hit the crossbar and post with two shots and then conspired to embarrass himself in front of the entire nation when sitting on the ball 2 yards from the line with the Swedish goalkeeper beaten. As he tried to scoop the ball into the net Clough fell awkwardly and sat on it: 'It looked like I'd laid the blasted thing,' he said.

Whether Clough was ever aware of the existence of Raynor's part in his career is hard to know. Certainly Raynor was not a subject in any of the biographies written under Clough's name, but Raynor's influence on Clough's career was nevertheless profound. From influencing the sale of Peter Taylor to Middlesbrough (without which the managerial partnership would never have existed) to writing the report that helped end Clough's international career (the ending of which, Clough always blamed on Winterbottom and which inversely inspired him to live his unmet potential through the success of his players).

Geoffrey Green in *The Times*' was highly critical of the technical deficiencies of the English players: '[Birmingham City's Trevor] Smith … at centre half … resembled some statue in a market place against the supreme flexibility and artistic touches of Simonsson.'

Two main ingredients seem to have been pertinent in the recipe for England's defeat. The first, brought about by the absence of Haynes, was the English forward line (the inside forward trio of Bobby Charlton, Jimmy Greaves and Clough) 'splitting up into single units', allowing the Swedish defence to close down and isolate the forwards; and the second, occurring in Sweden's second-half performance was '[Swedish] accuracy and inventiveness [which] gave them just that extra space and extra time that count.' Sweden won 3–2. To Raynor it was yet another sign that Englishfootball (even at the very top) was going backwards.

The presence of George Raynor at the post-game reception fascinated the press. How Raynor could now be plying his trade in the Midland League while aiding the defeat of England at Wembley came as something of a shock. He was interviewed and had this to say to the reporters:

> I feel like a football fifth columnist. I got some sort of satisfaction out of the result but not enough. I would much rather have been doing that same sort of thing for the country of my birth. All I consider is that the people in England have had their chance. I want to work in England. For England. They want me in Ghana, in Israel, in Mexico, and in Sweden. I am a knight in Sweden and have a huge gold medal of thanks from King Gustaf. I have a letter of thanks and commendation from the Prime Minister of Iraq. My record is the best in the world. I don't smoke. I don't drink. I live for football.

He spoke eloquently and at length with the FA grandees during the post-match reception. One suspects that Raynor was not aiming to upset people with blind criticism but to give an honest assessment as to why Sweden had won and how he would change things if he was given the chance.

There's no record as to whether this went down well or not but when interviewed later, Raynor stated that, presumably as a result of those discussions, he had been considered for the England manager's role that Ramsey was finally elected to undertake in 1963. And why wouldn't he have been? Of the candidates available at the time Raynor was the only one who had credentials as a coach in international football.

Certainly, the 3–2 result had got the Football Association thinking about what direction the national side should take, particularly in light of the fact that it was at the time busily canvassing support to host the 1966 World Cup, a decision ultimately conferred in August 1960. It would not have been misunderstood by the Football Association's hierarchy that if the intention was to either get England to the World Cup Final or avoid a national humiliation, then there was no Englishman more qualified than George Raynor to do so.

Prior to the immediate election of Winterbottom's successor there were, reportedly, only two men in the running for the No. 1 job in English football: Alf Ramsey and Jimmy Adamson. However, with regard to the international credentials of these candidates there was a poverty of choice. Adamson, who had led Burnley to the First Division title in 1960, had limited and patchy experience in coaching on the international stage. A fixture congestion certainly contributed to Burnley's defeat to Hamburg in the 1961 European Cup but even allowing for that, one could neither say that his influence as a coach to Walter Winterbottom in the 1962 World Cup was an unmitigated success (England were fortunate to qualify from their game after a near-elimination against Bulgaria in the final game) nor that his international experience amounted to much more than that.

Against that was the rise of Alf Ramsey. Ramsey had definitely landed on his feet when securing the manager's position at Ipswich Town because he was given time and shown respect enough to be allowed to get on with the job without undue interference from the directors of the club. Ramsey's reign at Portman Road, in that regard, compared favourably with that which Raynor experienced at Coventry City. The success of the Ipswich under Ramsey is undoubted but, here, again, was a man with limited experience beyond the confines of English football. In the 1963 European Cup, Ipswich had been eliminated as soon as the competition began in earnest. (Europe would have taken little interest in Ipswich walloping the Maltese champions in the early stages). In the next few months, after taking over as England manager, he took the national side to Paris for the return leg of a European Nations' Cup fixture.

England lost 5–2.

The concern for the press at the time was how blasé this new reign seemed. With one careless defeat Ramsey had immediately placed himself under pressure because before the World Cup finals in 1966, England would now have no more competitive fixtures. Privately, Ramsey revealed much when asking Jimmy Armfield, team captain in Paris that night, 'Is this the way England normally play?'

England's new manager had not even been bothered to run his eye over the national side before taking on the role.

As a candidate for international manager Ramsey was hardly ideal and, in retrospect, his wonderful legacy of winning the World Cup is mitigated by the regular disappointments that punctuated his tenure.

When surveying the Ramsey legacy, following the triumph of July 1966, David Miller wrote that 'instead of developing and expanding his new-found power and influence, Ramsey remained fundamentally cautious'. We can see this in a number of ways.

For a start, Ramsey was to show an alarming inability to vary tactics to suit the situation. In 1970 in Leon, during the quarter-final against West Germany Ramsey was tactically naive in his use of substitutes. For some reason, substitution for the sake of tactical advantage seemed a foreign concept to him.

He used it to rest players rather than bolster any apparent weakness in the team. At times this led to needless errors and a lack of tactical manoeuvring explains why left-back Terry Cooper (clearly knackered and confronted by Grabowksi the German substitute) was left on the field and Bobby Charlton (still full of running and providing a worthy opponent for Beckenbauer) was withdrawn. In 1972, against the same opponents, England needed

to overturn a 3–1 reverse in the Nations' Cup quarter-final in
Berlin, Ramsey selected a defensive midfield rather than an
attacking half-back line.

As a result England, pointlessly, drew the game 0–0.

At other important times, Ramsey was obdurate and inflexible.
In the 1973 World Cup qualifier against Poland, with time against
an England team in need of victory, Ramsey sat transfixed,
seemingly unable to conceive of an alternative plan of attack,
despite the fact that Poland were countering all English attacks.
On the bench beside him sat Bobby Moore, convincing him that
Kevin Hector should be sent on to attack the Poles down the
left side. When the change was finally made not only were there
just 90 seconds on the clock but Ramsey for whatever reason
dispensed with a forward (Chivers) to make way for Hector.

In addition, the embrace of foreign culture was never one of
Ramsey's fortes because his background was so unapologetically
British. He looked on foreigners with suspicion and contempt
and that would, at times, rebound on England. In 1963, in Rio,
he would find himself duped by age-old South American tactics
when Brazil delayed their arrival on the pitch during that year's
South American tour (Argentina did the same thing in the
1978 World Cup Final). The issue was not that Brazil delayed
their arrival, but that Ramsey instructed his side to enter the
field of play alone. Later, Ramsey contributed massively to the
unpopularity of England in Mexico in 1970 with his abrupt
attitude to local reporters and seemed to ignore the lessons from
his own history. Just why England were holed up in an inner-city
hotel (in easy car honking distance of the baying mob) prior to
the group match against Brazil in 1970 makes even less sense
when you consider that twenty years before Ramsey himself was
a member of the England party that stayed at the Luxor slap-bang
on the beachfront in Rio for the World Cup. The choice of both
hotels represented a failure to properly prepare for the World Cup.

One is struck, therefore, by the marked differences of Alf
Ramsey and George Raynor. Working overseas freed Raynor
from the reactionary and insular that characterise Ramsey.

Raynor did not have the luxury to ignore or avoid tactical developments; one could never say he was tactically inflexible. His decision to introduce a roving midfield schemer prior to the 1948 Olympics contrasts with his inventive containment of the Hungarians in 1953 and that, again, contrasts with his decision to sacrifice Liedholm in order to nullify the threat of Voinov during the quarter-final with Russia in 1958. Raynor, also, certainly learnt a great deal from carrying out sorties to the places where Sweden were to play in competitions. Staying in the Luxor Hotel and having his players eat indigestible hotel food was simply not going to happen to a team coached by George Raynor. Furthermore, Ramsey's reluctance to break up his one victorious team never occurred to Raynor. England's quarter-final exit to West Germany in 1970 can be laid at Ramsey's door, for he created a situation where Gordon Banks had ten times as much international experience as Peter Bonetti. Given the insistence on Sweden's FA to debar professional players from international selection we're not to know if Raynor would have shown a similar reluctance to change a winning team, but there is evidence enough to show that Raynor either altered line-ups to suit the situation (see the positional alterations introduced before the 1948 Olympics) or blooded youngsters into the team in order to safeguard continuous squad development.

One could say, therefore, that Raynor was the antithesis of Ramsey.

Once back in Skegness, Raynor was castigated for being a bit of a braggart, so qualified what he had said, explaining to the *Skegness Standard* that what he meant was: 'Because I said I have the best coaching record in the world does not mean that I am the best coach in the world.'

Perhaps, momentarily, Raynor personified the change in approach which English football needed to embrace if it wished to move on. What is definitely the case is that during the 1950s there had been a converse relationship between the rise of Raynor's stock and England's fall, particularly so when you compared England's lame performance in Sweden with Raynor's hugely respectable Final appearance.

It was a depressing decade for British international football, and writers from all sides were happy to verbalise the increasing dismay. The very titles of the football books written during that decade were reflective of a sense of national loss and bewilderment.

Hungary's victory in 1953 not only affected the way the game was played in Britain but the way the British viewed themselves.

In 1955, Brian Glanville's *Soccer Nemesis* was published, in which he charted the fall of English football. In 1956 Willy Meisl's *Soccer Revolution* appeared, emphasising the need for an evaluation as to how the game should be played in Britain. In 1959 Bernard Joy's *Soccer Tactics* and Kenneth Wolstenholme's *Young England* collectively put the boot in when surveying the disaster of England's 1958 World Cup campaign. In 1960 Stratton Smith edited the first edition of *World Soccer*, an attempt to cater for a growing British interest in foreign football. (How ironic! The most successful coach Britain had ever produced on the world stage, and yet the only time Raynor was ever to be mentioned in *World Soccer* (a magazine which reputedly had its finger on the pulse of the World Game) was in a two-paragraph obituary in 1985.)

Suddenly, in the weeks that followed the England v Sweden game, attention was directed toward Raynor, working quietly from his seaside bungalow and the mundane security of his non-league job.

Raynor became a figure who might hold the key to getting England out of the rut they found themselves in.

In November 1959 he was interviewed by Gerry Loftus for the *Sports Outlook* programme broadcast on Granada TV. Consider that: a prime-time national sports show featuring an interview with a non-league football coach.

That same month, Kenneth Wolstenholme, the BBC commentator then writing for the *Sunday Graphic* arrived in Skegness to ghost-write Raynor's autobiography *Football Ambassador at Large*, which Stanley Paul had commissioned. Wolstenholme was Raynor's favoured reporter as a result of the fact that he was the only English journalist to have given Sweden a chance before the World Cup Final. However, agreeing to have the book written in the first place proved to be a decision that Raynor would live to regret.

Wolstenholme's *Young England*, which had been published in 1959 by Stanley Paul, charted the Football Association's plan to develop potential young internationals into senior competitive internationals following the 1953 game against Hungary. However, rather than trumpeting the success of the programme, the ineptitude shown by England in the 1958 World Cup had caused such consternation at home that Wolstenholme had ended his book with a highly critical essay entitled 'An unhappy Swedish rhapsody'.

In that chapter, Wolstenholme states that there were three main reasons as to why things went so wrong in Gothenburg. Firstly, England arrived just days before the competition began. Secondly, when they did arrive they stayed in a 'plush' hotel with no training facilities for the squad and thirdly, the Football Association were inflexible in their approach to what we now refer to as 'squad rotation' – although they took twenty players, they played only the first eleven named in their squad during the group matches. It was in the play-off with the Soviet Union that 'reserves' would, incomprehensibly, be drafted into the team. (Indeed, some of the players in the play-off were actually making their international debuts!)

Wolstenholme was giving the public what he felt they wanted to hear. It may have been good for the sales of the book, but it was not a good strategy for Raynor to rely on such a candid writer if he were to harbour notions of currying favour with the Football Association of the day.

The book, when published in 1960, was called *Football Ambassador at Large*. Without question the Stanley Paul edition – withdrawn from sale in the first months of its publication – is the most important book in English football history.

It is half autobiography and half a blueprint for success. The book explains what Raynor had done in his career up to 1958, although taking management of Skegness Town is, perhaps understandably, omitted. Finally there are then three chapters which generally examine the reasons for British failure at World Cups.

The book presents a Raynor very different to the man who was so universally liked. Here he is outspoken and comes across both as a know-all and angry that the opportunity to use his ideas was being wasted: 'I am sorry that it has been impossible for me to get fixed up at home ... The thought of combining [management] with a job whereby I could put my knowledge and ideas to work helping English and British football attracts me. Apparently, however, it does not attract English and British football,' he wrote.

That barely concealed anger is not necessarily linked to the fact that Raynor was working at Skegness Town at the time. It was, however, linked to the fact that as a proud nationalist, Raynor was upset by the persistent failure of the Football Association to correct the course that the national side had taken through the progression of the previous three World Cups.

Raynor – or perhaps Wolstenholme putting words in his mouth – only 'states' what others had been thinking: '[winning] two games out of ten in the three World Cups ... is a record to be ashamed of ... a record that should herald some radical change in preparation.' Wolstenholme then betrays something of writer-client confidentiality when he recounts conversations Raynor had with figures at the highest levels in the game, in order to highlight the amateur preparation England had shown for World Cups and for the 1953 friendly versus Hungary. 'Walter Winterbottom once told me that English players don't like training camps ...' he wrote. Wolstenholme then has Raynor question whether England had bothered to prepare seriously for the World Cup in Brazil in 1950 as Sweden had by having Brazilian footballs and boots shipped over, and described the mishandling of that ill-fated World Cup attempt by the Football Association as 'sheer bad organisation'.

Wolstenholme goes on to report that Raynor felt that for the game against Hungary at Wembley in 1953, England (and by implication, the Football Association) 'were stricken with false impressions' and were naive in maintaining the belief that the Hungarians would come prepared to stop England rather than mount an attack against them. He adds that Raynor also queried whether England had the players to adopt the tactics that had so nearly seen Sweden beat Hungary in Budapest in November 1953.

In the chapter headed 'Where Britain Fails' Wolstenholme, under the guise of Raynor, presents five reasons for the failure of Britain to succeed at international level, and it is this criticism which the incumbent personnel at the Football Association would have felt particularly aggrieved about, because they could not escape the accusation that their lax preparation had contributed to the failure of the senior squad in the 1958 World Cup.

What is especially fascinating is the close similarity between Wolstenholme's arguments and phrasing in *Young England* and those comments which are attributed to Raynor in *Football Ambassador*, which leads me to suspect that 'Where Britain Fails' was a chapter written by Wolstenholme in Raynor's name. For instance, in both accounts Wolstenholme uses the word 'plush' to describe the Park Avenue Hotel where England's players stayed in Gothenburg, and also states that the players were referred to by the press pack as the 'Park Avenue Boys' – hardly a soubriquet Raynor would have been privy to.

This would of course explain the contradiction between Raynor proposing to Winterbottom that England use the Park Avenue Hotel (as Bob Ferrier remarked in Soccer Partnership) and Raynor now apparently criticising England for staying at the same hotel (as Brian Glanville draws on when writing that Raynor called it a 'sin and shame' that England stayed in Gothenburg).

Of the two versions, personally I believe that Ferrier's is the more credible.

If one chapter buried Raynor's hope of becoming the next England manager, then it was that one, because whereas whatever had happened in the 1950 World Cup was settled history, the people responsible for the debacle in Sweden were still very much in office when *Football Ambassador* was published.

Of course one would hope that Raynor would have seen the proofs and would have had an opportunity to contest what was written before the book was published, but my feeling is that Wolstenholme should have taken a more robust advisory role during the writing of the book and spelt out the possible consequences of the book being published in that form.

One feels that Raynor ruined his own career goal by putting his name to the book. Before it was published he was arguably the favourite to become the next England manager. Following the publication Raynor was quickly discarded from consideration.

During an interview with the *Skegness Standard* in December 1962, following the decision to appoint Alf Ramsey as England manager, Raynor let slip an interesting comment:

> I think my age might have had something to do with it. I'm 55 now and in their opinion, perhaps too old to take on such a big job [By comparison, Ramsey was 42, and Jimmy Adamson, the other candidate, was 33.] But I know I was well in the running. After all, my international coaching qualifications are better than any living Englishman. But my book didn't do me any good as far as the FA is concerned.

The book was, apparently, completed by January 1960 and published on 15 February 1960. Was it published in haste? Did Raynor have time to review the proofs? Ten thousand copies of the first edition were quickly sold. When Raynor was interviewed by the *Standard* following the publication he explained that he had only earned between £2,000 and £3,000 out of the book itself. He didn't seem that impressed by the amount but worse was to follow. In March 1960 publishers Stanley Paul received the first of several letters from lawyers representing various members of the Football Association threatening Raynor with libel, and demanding that the book be withdrawn from sale. It is impossible to find the Stanley Paul edition of the book for sale.

Ironically, the revision of the book (published by Soccer Book Club) now attracts ridiculous price tags online.

After taking advice from the publisher, Raynor agreed to their demands. Stanley Paul quickly sold the rights, in order to recoup their losses, to The Soccer Book Club. They took the decision to remove or significantly alter the twenty-two paragraphs from the original publication that were the cause of such litigious commotion, and printed the book otherwise in its entirety. It may have had less appeal with the controversial paragraphs excised, but it still represented a blazing criticism of the national game and how things could be corrected.

Why the most important book in English football history? In answering this question it is important to note that at the time Walter Winterbottom was undertaking the dual role of Director of Coaching and England team manager. Some criticisms of Winterbottom are that his role involved more than he could undertake, others that his primary interest was in coaching rather than managing the England team.

The former role was one which encompassed a nationwide brief, and the role of national director was very much inkeeping with the work that Raynor had successfully undertaken in Sweden. When Alf Ramsey was elected to the position of England team manager, he clearly did not favour taking on the role of Director of Coaching for this was removed from Ramsey's remit and handed to Allen Wade. One could argue that coaching thus became a secondary consideration compared to the role of England manager and the focus of the national side itself.

One then gets into the area of conjecture. If Raynor had been elected to the position of team manager then it is most likely that he would have sought to keep both roles, particularly in light of his experiences and successes in Sweden in overseeing coaching policy. Where this would have got England is impossible to guess but the descent of the England team from World Cup winners in 1966, to Bronze medallists in the European Nations Cup in 1968, to the complete failure to qualify for the

European Championships in 1972, the World Cup in 1973 and succeeding tournaments is hardly reflective of successful strategic planning.

Compare that, however, with the successes of the Swedes between 1948 and 1958 and the programmes that the Swedish FA introduced to overcome problems they faced and it becomes somewhat apparent that a Raynor-led England may have led the national side away from the continued failures that have beset the national side after 1966.

Of course Raynor did not lead England and (if he is to be believed) the book is the reason for that. By that reasoning the book opened the way for Ramsey and the triumph of 30 July 1966.

But so too did the book open the door for the negativity that surrounded Ramsey's management style and closed the door on a strategic national coaching programme: the type that had reaped such rewards for Sweden; the type that was evidently far beyond the conception of the Football Association and the resources given to Allen Wade. It meant twelve years in the wilderness for the England football team after 1970. It meant constant failure that now manifests itself in the widespread belief that the national side have little if any chance of actually winning international competitions despite an overabundance of coaches at all levels.

Nevertheless, it is an interesting pursuit considering what might have happened if Stanley Paul had never set out to publish the autobiography of George Raynor.

17

DISPUTE

In early 1960 George started working at the Derbyshire Miners' Welfare Home, a complex of buildings near Winthorpe. During that year the National Union of Mineworkers were investing a great deal of money in the development of the home, which offered respite for ex-miners. Exactly what work George undertook there is not known. George Crawford, a local resident and goalkeeper for Skegness Town who was employed at that time to help in the development of the Home, recalled George working there but could not recall what he was doing, although Ian Chadband, writing in the *Evening Standard* in 2002, stated that George was teaching English to Hungarian mineworkers who had fled their homeland following the 1956 uprising in their country.

Around the same time, in January 1960, the Swedish Football Association made another attempt at persuading Raynor to go back to coach the national side. The work he was doing at Skegness Town, though dear to his heart, was evidently not to everyone's liking. Within the club, officials were privately voicing concerns to Harold Swift that the club was not progressing as quickly as they believed it should. Such comments were at the time kept within the club, but Raynor was evidently aware

of what was being said and agreed to a new contract with the
Swedish Football Association which would keep him in Sweden
from May to November of 1960. Interviewed by the *Skegness
Standard*, Harold Swift informed the reporter that there was little
he could have done in the face of the offer from Stockholm.
However, he denied rumours that Raynor had left because the
club had given him no cash to buy players, and was comforted
by the fact that he would be saving £500 in wages.

Raynor had also received offers from Rotherham, Grimsby
and Scunthorpe and from non-league Cambridge City, but
he refused all of them and headed back to Stockholm to help
prepare the Swedes for the 1962 World Cup. The Swedes had
been drawn with the Belgians and Swiss in the European
Qualifying Group One, and were perhaps fortunate to play
Belgium in October 1960 before the young side had found
their form. Under his guidance Sweden won all but one
of their games that season, with only Norway beating them,
in Oslo. Accordingly, Sweden had made a good start to their
World Cup campaign.

Raynor's return to Skegness now carried an air of unreality.
Although the club was no longer even playing in the Midland
League, was having to put pressure on referees to play games
when the pitch was waterlogged (as the players' wages still had
to be met, regardless) and was having to rely on Raynor to make
up the numbers on occasion, some of the best young players
in Sweden were travelling over to Skegness just to be coached
by Raynor. That meant that Skegness Town, struggling to find
£20 to pay their players, now found themselves in the unlikely
situation of being able to play the right-winger from Orebro,
Rolf Viberg, and the Swedish Under-23 international Tord
Grip at inside right.

The case was even more bizarre when it came to Grip
(who later became the assistant to Sven Goran Eriksson when
he was the England manager), for Aston Villa had arranged
a series of trials for the player. Famous old Aston Villa turned
down in favour of Skegness Town!

Raynor's views were still being sounded out elsewhere. In January 1961 he was paid to travel up to Scotland and report on a Scottish League match between Hearts and Dundee and wrote an article that was evidently warmly received by the press: 'Too many runners, two few strategists,' he wrote, explaining on his arrival back in Yorkshire that many readers had thanked him for articulating that which they had been unable to express themselves.

In March 1961 Raynor went back to Sweden to complete the qualifying matches in preparation for the World Cup in Chile. His first game in charge of the Swedish team in 1946 had seen him pitting his wits against Karl Rappan, the coach of Switzerland. Now, in 1961 he would meet Rappan again, who once more was coaching the Swiss team. Unfortunately, Raynor and Sweden would also experience the flip side of the luck that had been theirs all those years ago.

That Sweden would not qualify for the World Cup in 1962 was, at one point, unthinkable. For their second game in the group, the Swedes played Switzerland, and completely dominated them 4–0 to move comfortably to the top of the group. The team, which now included Agne Simonsson (playing in Spain) and Ingvar Brod (playing in France), seemed to be performing perfectly well and there were high hopes for the future. One event which possibly escaped attention in Stockholm following the game against Switzerland was the decision to lift the ban on Heinz Schneiter. He had been sent off when playing for Switzerland in the game against Sweden and his appeal against the expulsion was upheld.

That summer, the correspondent reporting for the *FA Yearbook* was already confidently predicting that Sweden would qualify for the finals. In October 1961, as if to emphasise the point, the Swedes travelled to Belgium for their first away game and once again recorded a marvellous victory, with Ingve Brod scoring both goals in a 2–0 victory. Had the group been decided on goal difference, that 2–0 victory would have assured Sweden's qualification; however, points determined the winners of each group and if there was a tie on points, then a play-off would determine qualification. This meant that Sweden now needed only to avoid defeat in their away game in Switzerland to qualify for the finals in Chile.

Raynor once more campaigned for Simonsson's inclusion and this faith was rewarded with a 1st-minute goal. Inside 10 minutes, however, outside left Charles Antenen, who had played in both the 1950 and 1954 World Cup finals, scored an equaliser for Switzerland. Rolf Wuthrich then put the Swiss in the lead, before Ingve Brod equalised for Sweden with a quarter of an hour to go. That appeared to be enough for Sweden but with just minutes to go Eschmann struck the winner for Switzerland.

The Swiss, fearful of a late equaliser, then started to employ all manner of tactics to slow the game down. Even the spectators joined in, kicking the ball away when it was punted into the crowd and then, in the final minute, just as Lennart Backman was placing the ball to take a corner for Sweden, a spectator came onto the field and grabbed the ball out of his hands.

There would need to be a play-off to determine the group winner, and FIFA determined that it should take place in West Berlin. Memories of the 1958 World Cup semi-final, when Germany felt they had been harshly treated in losing the game to Sweden, were still fresh. This immediately gave the Swiss an advantage, for the 'neutral' German crowd were hardly friendly to the Swedes. The game was played in appalling conditions, with the ground being sodden due to a downpour before kick-off.

Despite this, Sweden got off to a fine start, and Brod's first-half goal was scored from fully 30 yards when the Swiss defender Tachella played a loose back pass to his goalkeeper Elsener, and Brod smashed the ball straight into the net.

Schneiter's reprieve from suspension now told. In the second half he advanced to head home a shot from Eschmann. This firmly tipped the balance away from Sweden,

and encouraged by the crowd, Switzerland got stronger as the
game progressed. With a quarter of an hour to go Allemann's
corner was headed home by Antenen.

Sweden were out.

When Raynor returned to Skegness in November 1961 –
Skegness had now won the Central Alliance – it was with some
surprise that he did so, for he had no job to come back to.
In his absence he had received offers from the Danish Football
Association to help coach Denmark at the Tokyo Olympics,
AIK in Stockholm and offers from Football League clubs but
rather than taking any of them up, he was instead returning
to Skegness where his position at the club was at best as
unpaid honorary manager to Norman Chase. In December
he explained the reasons underlying this decision to the
local press:

> I just want to make my roots here. A job as a welfare officer or youth
> work is what I want. If I can get something like that in the Skegness
> district I will give my spare time to helping Skegness Town, as I have
> done before. I am an idealist. Whether it's Sweden in the World Cup or
> Skegness Town juniors it's all football to me. I believe we must start at the
> bottom if Britain is to recapture her place in world sport.

He was true to his word: workday evenings would see him
happily conducting training under the lights of the Embassy car
park in the town centre. When interviewed, he said:

> There is a great deal of difference between football fitness and general
> fitness. A player must be able to last the full 90 minutes. Charlie Williams
> is one who can. Five-a-sides, short sprints and particularly speed off the
> mark form a major part of the training session. No footballer plays at one
> pace throughout a game, so his training must be adapted to enable him
> to make the sudden effort without difficulty.

In February 1962 Raynor made a short visit to Sweden and
when he returned to England he applied for the position of a

bathing pool superintendant at Butlins. This might have seemed a move of desperation, but Raynor remained altruistic in his leanings and wished to stay close to the town, remarking:

> The irony of the matter is that there are plenty of big jobs waiting for me elsewhere. [He continued to receive offers from Football League clubs including Watford, Scunthorpe, Carlisle, Notts Forest and Rochdale, and from non-League clubs Cambridge City and Rugby.] But I do not want a big job, just something small so that I can stay in Skegness and get cracking on some of the things I want to do. I want to re-open the football school, then re-form the Skegness A team and generally encourage local youths to take greater interest in sport.

It was clear that Skegness Town was beginning to see the benefits of Raynor's attempts to bring in young players through to the first team. In March 1962, five members of the old A team were in the Midland League side versus Stamford, with one of them, Mick French, scoring twice from the wing in the 3–0 win.

Raynor's application for the bathing pool job was unsuccessful, but in March he found alternative work in a small engineering plant at Alford. He did eventually get a job at Butlins, as the Sports Equipment Supervisor and later became the assistant manager there on a seasonal contract until 1967. Raynor's relationship with Skegness Town throughout that period continued to remain close. Following the dismissal of player-manager Jimmy Maddison, Raynor was re-employed as club manager in March 1963 after a committee meeting at which he outlined his new plans for the club. This included changing the training scheme 'on a scale hitherto unimagined' based, he said, on the systems founded and sponsored by the big Continental clubs.

These plans were grand and sophisticated but Raynor was preaching to the wrong audience. The tight finances of the club meant that, as the *Skegness Standard* explained, 'Many of his suggestions fell on deaf ears'. Raynor pushed them through regardless. George Crawford, the goalkeeper for the club at the time, remembered:

George Raynor ruined Skegness Town Football Club! We used to have
a lottery at the club: 'a shilling a week' which would pay for the general
outgoings of the club. When George came the spend started to increase
so much because when we travelled to North Shields, up to Gateshead
and the Newcastle area we would start to stay overnight at hotels there.
Before [that time] we would travel on the day and return after the game.
Suddenly we were heading up the night before. Financially, the club
couldn't stand it.

The result was self-defeating. Raynor was advising that more
money be spent, but Swift and Cooke simply didn't have the
cash available to invest in the type of players required to enable
the club to advance from the Midland League. Mick French,
also drafted into the first team around this time, recalls the very
bizarre spectacle of Skegness travelling by train to a Midland
League game in the north-east in first class, while back in
the economy car the Arsenal players were heading up to play
Newcastle United!

Even so, Crawford had sympathy for Raynor:

George Raynor was not given enough cash to do anything really. When
I went to Worksop for their Midland League Championship year in
1965/66, money was not a problem. I was paid over three times there
what I was earning at Skegness. I think that Harold Swift and his business
partner, Geoff Cooke, were intent to put a bit of cash into the club but it
was never enough to secure the type of footballers that you really need
to succeed at any level. We had a poor team, as a result, and were always
in the bottom four or five.

Whatever his thoughts on other aspects, Crawford had nothing
but praise for Raynor as a coach:

George was a superb coach, though. He would take me to one side and
say 'do this or do that' and when you started doing what he said you
realised just what worth there were in those ideas. It really put things
into perspective for you and really brought your game on. He got the

wingers to step over the ball when they were on the attack. That was
not really a feature of the game in those days but it was effective.
He brought over ideas that we had not seen. He took me under his wing.
He told me, genuinely, that I could play for England. He secured me a
trial with Southampton to see Ted Bates but that didn't work out and
then I went (also on his say) to Watford who were coached by Ronnie
Burgess. But the set up there for the trainees was not ideal. I was there
for four days and no one had bothered to show up to see me play in the
trial games and there was another young Irish goalkeeper there at the
time and I remember saying to him, 'stuff this, I can't be messed about.
I'm going home.' The Irish lad turned to me and said 'I can't go home,
I've got to stay.' That was Pat Jennings.

George Crawford remained at Skegness for four seasons, up to
1965, and appeared to be a favourite with Raynor, who kept
back a young Ray Clemence (the future England goalkeeper) as
Crawford's understudy. Finally, frustrated at a lack of opportunity
to get into the first team, Clemence would soon move across
to Midland League rivals Notts County before heading onto
Scunthorpe United. 'We were able to pick up some good
players. One, of course, was Charlie Williams. He had played for
Doncaster Rovers, but by the time we had him his knees had
gone for top league football – but he was still quick, was Charlie,'
Crawford remembered. He continued:

But without the money to attract the players [George Raynor] was up
against it. If he had been at Worksop with their budget we would have won
the league every year. They had good former League players there, from
Barnsley, Doncaster and Rotherham. They had real quality there. George
did not have those resources at Skegness at any time so it is not surprising
that he did not achieve any success with the club. I think George, to be
honest, was his own man. He wanted things his way or no way. What he
said, went. That may have been one of the problems for him. At Skegness
he did not have the same type of interference from Harold Swift that he
would have got from other owners at the clubs and in some ways that is
why he never went from Skegness to another Midland League club.

At Skegness, George showed himself to still have that common touch: 'You could tell he was an advanced coach,' said Mick French, 'but what always struck me was the way he would encourage everyone; he treated everyone the same, regardless of their talent.' In another interview, French also said of him, 'If George was ever bitter about his lot, he never showed it. He was a gentleman, generous and never made it seem as if the job was beneath him.'

By May 1963 the *Skegness Standard* remarked that Raynor's influence had turned the club around, and in the last few months of the season Skegness had beaten the league leaders Loughborough 3–1 away, of which Raynor remarked: 'It was a tactical victory, based on the counter-attack principle. It was just a question of neutralising them.' But his arrival had come too late to avert a low finish that season. The *Standard* was pleased overall though, with the change in the attitude of the personnel, a change that Raynor had instigated. Of the young full-back Weldon Richardson, the *Standard* wrote that 'his poised confidence has taken the place of clumsy enthusiasm'. Meanwhile, Mick Brealey had developed into 'a personality player', and as for goalkeeper Crawford, the star from Louthhad become 'the most highly rated of the keepers in the league'.

As time went on, it became increasingly more obvious that Swift and Cooke simply did not have the cash to fund theirs and Raynor's dreams. In August 1963, Raynor caused a minor revolt when he dropped a player who refused to play without guarantees of a win bonus. As likely signings turned their backs on the club, so it suffered on the pitch. It took 8 games for the club to record their first win of the 1963/64 season and Skegness were now fighting to hold onto their prized possession, George Crawford, who was becoming the target of interest from league clubs. In one appearance, at Worksop in November 1964, he was cheered off by the home supporters (even though Skegness went down 4–0) such was his performance in keeping the rest of the shots out.

Raynor started resorting to any method to arrest the slide the club were on. A pitiful start to the new campaign had Raynor scratching around for any plan to stop the poor patch of form that the club found themselves in. In November 1964, against Lockheed, he experimented with a 7–0–3 formation, explaining that 'the goalie has seven defenders directly in front of him and three forwards (insides and centre). The wingers mark their opposite numbers following them back when needed until they can hand over to the full-backs. The halves must control the middle of the field, mainly for defence.' It was hardly a roaring success since the club only drew 0–0 but at least it had stopped the rot.

Such desperation hardly manifested itself into a successful season.

Clearly, the writing was on the wall. In August 1965 he called in a favour from Doncaster Rovers – Raynor had contributed significantly to getting Alick Jeffrey back into Rovers' professional ranks – and Rovers acceded to a request for Burgh Road to bring their first team over for a pre-season friendly. A solid handshake photo-opportunity of the two signalled a genuine respect between Raynor and his previous charge. Such stunts weren't enough and by September 1965 the directors of the club were gathering to signal a lack of confidence in Raynor and his methods.

Conscious of the problems at the club, the *Skegness Standard* confronted Raynor about the rumours that all was not well. He said, 'There's no smoke without fire. I left previously because of the critics. You can't win matches without key players, and you can't sign key players without money. Whoever does the job after me will soon find that out. The fact is that I have increased demands of my time at Butlins as the Chief Storeman and players from outside the area are making organising training difficult.' The mood was not brightened when the club lost heavily to Grantham in the FA Cup that autumn.

In November 1965 Raynor resigned.

18

THE DESCENT

In 1967 Raynor was to return to league management, a move which was inspired by England's dramatic victory in the World Cup the previous year. After leaving Skegness Town, like the rest of country, he had become magnetised by the 1966 World Cup in which Alf Ramsey became the second English coach to lead a side to a World Cup final.

It was a remarkable achievement on the part of Ramsey and his team, who faced the very best opposition on their way to victory. There were no easy matches after England's qualification from Group 1. Argentina were likely winners, far stronger that year than Brazil. Portugal's side were formed from the famous Benfica side that were succeeding in Europe at the time, while West Germany, on the verge of their domination of Europe in the early 1970s, were formidable opponents in the final.

Yet England defeated each of them.

England had an incredibly close shave against Argentina, who fielded a side with players widely accepted to be far better than those of the English team: yet England won because Ramsey stuck to his guns, unshakeable in his belief that adherence to a system could bring success.

England's success fascinated Raynor. Ramsey had achieved something incredible: other countries had better players, but he had masked deficiencies by creating a solid club side – the team was the thing. After the final, Raynor was interviewed by *Sunday Times* journalist Stephen Fay. It was a short article, which charted the remarkable rise of England from the nadir of November 1953 to the splendour of that summer afternoon in July 1966, when the whole country had been united in appreciation of what had been achieved. Ladies could be heard discussing team selections in the hair salons, and the interminable chat on the buses was all about football. Yet there was Fay, willing to include a short, punchy statement from Raynor which tempered the mood and provided a conscientious appraisal regarding the victory. Raynor told Fay: 'There is in football no substitute for skill … but the manager's job is usually to try to find one. Ramsey obviously found one.'

It was a quote that said a great deal about Raynor's recognition, along with Ramsey's, that individuality had to be subsumed in the interests of a cohesive unit if the team was to achieve success. It was a lesson he had learned all those years before at Gigg Lane, and was the premise upon which all of Sweden's triumphs had been staged. It was a lesson upon which England achieved their single triumph, and one which was to bring Raynor back into the footballing fold.

It was the intervention of Frank Wilson, the managing director of a tyre manufacturer in the Doncaster area, and the newly appointed chairman of Doncaster Rovers, which brought Raynor back into the professional ranks of the Football League on 9 June 1967. Interviewed at the time, Wilson said, 'We decided on Mr Raynor because of his vast experience. We think we have the players. Mr Raynor has the knowledge.' It was not the most secure of managerial appointments – Raynor would become Rovers' eleventh manager in eleven years – but it gave him one of those challenges that he found so irresistible in life. The previous incumbent Keith Kettleborough, who had only been in the post for five months, had presided over the club's relegation into the Fourth Division, so here was a splendid opportunity for Raynor to turn around the fortunes of the club.

At Doncaster, Raynor renewed his association with Alick Jeffrey, who had returned to the club in the mid-1960s and had scored fairly regularly ever since. George's impact on the club was instantaneous, slicing two weeks off the players' summer holiday and asking them to report in the first week in July 1967. His renown for pre-planning was evident in his need for an early start: 'We must have a thorough preparation for the first match. There is work to be done, points to be ironed out, and we must start as we mean to go on,' he said and to substantiate his intentions, moved his family to Ambassador Gardens, in Armthorpe, near Doncaster.

Early season form was patchy; the players the club had were not up to the standard needed to push the club toward the promotional spots. In November 1967 the club lost away to Rochdale and the players were treated to a bollocking from Frank Wilson, storming into the away dressing room on completion of the match to give his full and frank appraisal of their performance. He then met with Raynor in an emergency meeting and as a result of that meeting Wilson accepted that the cheque book would have to come out. Armed with said cheque book, Raynor now did a remarkable bit of trade that secured Doncaster's short-term future.

At Rotherham United (managed at that time by Tommy Docherty) Raynor identified three experienced professionals who he knew could do a good job for him at Rovers and around whom he could select younger players. This strategy of forming a nucleus of experience in the side and then using that to develop the club when adding inexperienced players to the side was the same as that which he had pursued with Sweden with such success in similar circumstances. The three players were Harold Wilcockson, Colin Clish, an attacking defender, and Chris Rabjohn. Raynor traded two teenagers for their services: Dennis Leigh, and the forward, Graham Watson. The fortunes of the respective clubs proved who had done the better deal. Whereas Rotherham finished twenty-first that year and were relegated, Doncaster kicked on, lost only 3 of their last 19 matches and attracted some excellent late season gates in addition: 12,000 at home to Darlington; 10,000 at home to Port Vale, and nearly 9,000 to see Bradford City, a testament to the standard and style of play with which Raynor encouraged in his team.

Raynor prepared the players for the second season in the same methodical way as the previous one, but it was a gruelling regime for a 60 year old. The first few games went well with 9 wins in the first 14 matches (the club became a magnet for youngsters seeking a breakthrough: one young lad, Kevin Keegan, being turned away at the door of Belle Vue thus never meeting the equally diminutive Raynor), but by early November the fans and the press had been witness to a run of poor form. The *Doncaster Evening Post* reporter Joe Slater wrote that a few weeks previously 'I could sit in the Press box at away matches and tell the "home" journalists with reasonable expectations of it coming true, that the only question about the game was how many goals Rovers would win by.'

Suddenly, the team lost both full-backs to injury and in 4 matches shipped 11 goals. Raynor had neither the energy nor the luck to alter the downward course. 'They reached a real low at Wrexham,' wrote Slater, continuing, 'and that opinion is shared by the club's chairman, Mr Frank Wilson, who told me after that game that he rated Rovers' performance on a par with the one at Rochdale last season ... the match which preceded the famous "pep talk" to his men.'

On 2 November 1968, the side lost ineptly to Lincoln City at home. Slater wrote on 4 November that 'the present run of failure where success has been so expected is leading to tenseness and desperation where once there was coolness and thought.' Such comments could not have alleviated Raynor's difficulties in seeking not only to bring about results but also to encourage entertaining football.

On 4 November 1968, the draw for the first round of the FA Cup pitched Rovers at home to Notts County, and Raynor declared himself to be well content with the draw. However, at the home game the following Wednesday there was yet more depression: 'The slow handclap once again rang around Belle Vue,' wrote Slater. 'Yet who can blame the fans, who have now seen a series of matches almost defying description.' Such was the gloom that Raynor handed in his notice the following day, although he would remain for a short while longer as coach and trainer to the youth side.

On 8 November the *Doncaster Evening Post* included the full statement from Frank Wilson, the chairman to explain the sudden loss of the club's manager. The epitaph of George Raynor's football career in England was fifteen paragraphs in length, and closed with the following words: 'Let me pay tribute to a gentleman of football. Quietly dignified, purposeful and knowledgeable and a credit to his profession. George Raynor, international coach, associate of Doncaster Rovers. May we have the privilege of your advice for a long time to come. Good wishes from all of us at Belle Vue for your future.'

On 9 November, Slater recounted how Raynor explained to the players that he was stepping down, telling them, 'I've dropped myself'. It transpired that Raynor had been thinking of resigning for some time and had wanted to leave the club at the top of the table but it just hadn't worked out like that. Slater remarked:

> It wasn't a sacking or a retirement – something that Belle Vue had grown used to. This time it was altogether different. The matter was openly discussed over a cup of coffee. All very friendly. And there probably lies the crux of Mr Raynor's problems – problems which have only recently come to the fore after a great run. He is just too friendly. Too much of a nice guy, where too many players need a strong disciplinarian, I don't know anybody who doesn't like George Raynor. He is, as Mr Wilson rightly said, 'a gentleman of soccer'. I have always felt that the more the people under someone in charge dislike – even hate – their boss, the more and better will be their output … In addition Raynor has also been a victim of his own attacking football policy in an endeavour to give the public more adventurous soccer to watch.

George's replacement was the former Gateshead player Lawrie McMenemy. Nearly half his age, McMenemy was a former guardsman who brought the enthusiasm of youth and military bearing to the job, two characteristics that the club was in desperate need of. McMenemy, with Raynor's squad of players, would win the Fourth Division title the same season.

McMenemy remembers:

> George was a nice fella. By the time I'd turned up he had turned 60. I do remember that he came to see me and had a cup of tea with me. I welcomed it, him coming to see me, because he had been in the game so long. He wasn't bitter at all but wished me all the best. He gave me some general advice and told me to look out for this and that. You know. The one thing that struck me about George though was that there was no edge to him. It certainly helped me arriving at Doncaster when I did. When I went to Southampton, you see, Ted Bates [who had been at Southampton for many years] had resigned; now it would have been different if [Bates] had been forced out because I would have had to have won over the players there. But at Doncaster, George had brought in a lot of new players and so there was none of the comparisons with the old and new managers that could have gone on. The players I inherited from George did a good job for me, players like Colin Clish and John Bird.

Thereafter Raynor busied himself helping schools in Doncaster. He became vice-chairman of the Doncaster Coaching Association and maintained a connection with Sweden, regularly visiting the country and dropping in on the clubs and players he had worked with. However, George's health started to deteriorate. Rheumatism had started to affect him greatly as he aged, and by 1970, two writers from Aftonbladet who went to visit him in Doncaster were, moreover, shocked by the sadness of him. At the time he was living on sickness benefits: gone was the lively, ever-smiling character who had been popularised in Swedish print and media. There he sat, surrounded by a dusty collection of medals, commemorative trinkets and his knight's order. 'The only thing I'm rich in,' he said, 'are my memories.'

News reached Sweden, and Bertil Nordahl started a fund for George and his wife, which at least enabled him to continue travelling over to Sweden in order to reacquaint himself with the football and footballers there.

In the 1970s other Englishmen found work in Sweden, amongst them Alan Ball Snr, Bobby Houghton and Roy Hodgson, and the effect of Raynor was still much in evidence even then.

Current England manager, Roy Hodgson, who has done so well overseas and at home and maintains a marvellous dignity in all his dealings, remembers: 'I met George once or twice during the 1970s and found him to be both likeable and knowledgeable as one would expect. He commanded respect in the Swedish football fraternity ... but I never really got the impression that George, as coach, got any real credit for [his] achievements.'

In 1972, Raynor recalled his first visit to Sweden in 1946 in a newspaper interview, and used the forum to draw a comparison with what he saw in the English game in the early 1970s when such players as Ron 'Chopper' Harris, and Norman 'Bite Yer Legs' Hunter characterised a less cerebral approach which English, indeed world football, had then embraced (during the 1974 World Cup he had been asked about the Brazilian defence in preparation for the 'semi-final' versus Holland: 'Brazil's back four ... is defensively the best in the competition. Holland will find it very difficult to score,' he'd said. As it transpired the game descended into a beastly brawl; one Brazilian being sent off and two others booked). Raynor goes on to say:

> [English football] has always relied on strength. Technically English footballers are a long way behind their Continental counter-parts. When I went to Sweden after the war everybody could bend the ball with either side of the foot. Today English football is played by marathon runners, and yet nobody can run as fast as the ball can be played. Accurate passing and intelligent positioning, these are the essential parts of the game. Economy of effort. It's not new, just a question of applying it.

He still felt that the coaching of footballers was a simple matter made hard: 'Teaching football is all about teaching technique,' he said.

George developed Alzheimer's disease in later life. Sid Raynor remembers him once more coming to Hoyland and seeing him chatting away to a lady buying some chips, only to inadvertently ignore Sid, unable to recognise his own nephew.

Brian and his parents moved to Buxton in Derbyshire soon after, where George was eventually moved to the Derby House Nursing Home, a family-run residential home for the elderly. Raynor's Alzheimer's condition was linked to the cerebral vascular disease that would ultimately kill him.

He died on 11 November 1985. There was no obituary notice printed in *The Times*, the *Daily Telegraph* or anywhere else in the national press. In November, Brian Hide, Wesleyan lay preacher at the same chapel where Raynor first attended Bible Classes and where he married Phyllis, received a call from a Mrs Shaw who lived in Elsecar.

She informed Brian that the family's request was to have a short thanks-giving service in front of 'two or three' friends at the Wesleyan Chapel, and for George's ashes to be interned in the churchyard of Trinity Church in Elsecar. And there he rests. Along the pathway from the grave of Sir Thomas Tomlinson, across from the joyful playground sounds of the local primary school, down the road from the mouth of the pit where his father worked and a 5-minute tramp from the muddy path to that overgrown football pitch on Furnace Hills where it all began for George Raynor.

AFTERWORD

In many respects George Raynor was no different from a number of pre-war footballers who successfully plied their trade coaching footballers in Europe. Like them, he gained his apprenticeship in league football during a period when individual technique and ball control were seemingly of a higher value than they are today. Those men were valued by communities who had an insatiable desire to learn from the originators of the game.

Raynor was no different, say, to Jimmy Hogan, who did so much to successfully promote an excellence in coaching and football in Central Europe in the 1930s and this had a direct positive influence on the great Austria side of the 1930s and the Hungary side of the 1950s. Raynor was likewise no different to Lesley Lievesley, the coach of the great Turin side of the 1940s which did so much to shape Italian football during and after the war; no different to Frank Soo who did so much to help develop the game in Sweden in 1950s.

Indeed, there were a vast number of British ex-professional footballers who contributed globally to the development of the game abroad and built up that rapport and affection for the love of the British game which still exists in some measure today.

The game itself owes a debt of gratitude to those individuals who presented such a gift to the world. Raynor was not different, really, to any of those individuals in that regard.

How Raynor did differ was in terms of his success at national level with Sweden.

Raynor liked to trumpet these successes to the British as a way of publicising his talent to the land of his birth, he was also conscious that for England to improve they would need to deconstruct the game they had been taught to play: to accept fundamental criticisms and start considering matters afresh. A true patriot, Raynor was critical but constructive with his criticism.

In the end the British never really understood just what he had achieved in Sweden and never really understood him.

In England he was offered employment in the Third Division and the Midland League, despite achieving the type of World Cup and international success that the English, in particular, have long since pined for. Even today it is embarrassing to compare his record at World Cups with that of Sir Alex Ferguson, Ron Greenwood, Sven Goran Erikson, Jock Stein, Sir Bobby Robson and Fabio Capello.

Brian Glanville remarked in his *Soccer Nemesis* that nowhere else but in England would such a Titan of European football be found employment in the third tier of domestic football. Sad to say but that was the very height of Raynor's managerial involvement with domestic football in England.

To understand what he achieved in Sweden one must understand Swedish football in the 1940s and 1950s. During Raynor's first spell coaching the national side between 1946 and 1953, Sweden would only allow amateurs to play the game in their country: players were not paid to play. It would be wrong, however, to say that the players were not motivated by money in those days, and many were quite happy to leave Sweden to play professionally during that period. The lack of money in the game in Sweden definitely limited the pool of players which Sweden could call on, but on the plus side it did create an environment in which players committed themselves wholeheartedly to the game, and it was amongst those types of the players that Raynor thrived. His enthusiasm fed hundreds of devoted students and the game really took off in Sweden as a result.

Rather than drawing comparisons between the triumphs of the Swedish national side and those of the professional national sides of the era, their achievements should be measured against other amateur sides of the same period. In this regard 'Sweden' were way ahead of other teams. They won one Olympic Gold medal in 1948 and even with a severely weakened side would most probably have added another Gold medal in Helsinki in 1952 if the IOC and FIFA had taken robust action against the sham amateurism promoted by the Eastern bloc in the 1950s. This saw national sides throughout Eastern Europe play as amateur players when they were nothing of the sort. The governments of Hungary and Yugoslavia, to name but two examples, would simply underwrite the expenses of their players and teams and provide such as to fundamentally promote the opportunities for their national teams.

Against other genuinely amateur sides of the Raynor era, 'Sweden' were clearly supreme, winning the Olympic Gold medal at London in 1948, the Olympic Bronze medal at Helsinki in 1952 and the Nordic Championship in 1953 – but they also punched well above their weight against the best professional sides of the time too. They rattled an excellent England team in 1947 in England, then beat them comprehensively in Stockholm, followed by overturning the odds to defeat the Republic of Ireland in Dublin in 1949. They defeated Italy and Spain during the World Cup, in 1950 came agonisingly close to upsetting the Uruguay side during the final group stage of the same competition, and gave Hungary an almighty scare in Budapest in November 1953.

Remember that these were all matches in which Sweden's genuinely amateur players (firemen, pastry chefs, teachers) were playing against full-time professional footballers.

These successes were not achieved in spite of Raynor, but were achieved because of Raynor. He was the one who truly inspired confidence and gave belief to the players, and he was the one who created the environment within which the players developed and succeeded.

You may have noticed that earlier I used inverted commas when writing that 'Sweden' were arguably way ahead of other teams. This is because the Swedish team that won the 1948 Olympic Gold (and which could have challenged the dominance of the fabulous Hungary side if they had been kept together) was only one of a number of Swedish teams Raynor coached.

He coached that side for two years from 1946 to the end of 1948, after which the side was broken up as players left to join professional clubs throughout the Continent.

Within a short period of time Raynor developed new incarnations of the Swedish national team, cobbling together seniors and youth players to form sides that, impressively, could still compete with some of the best teams in the world. As an instance of this, the team that came very close to inflicting a home defeat on mighty Hungary in November 1953 was really no more than a fourth string Sweden XI that had been formed during the course of that 2-game tour. It was Raynor's ideas and coaching that caused that team to come so close to causing one of the biggest upsets in football history.

His successes were based on several key factors: firstly, by being open to the resources, opinions and ideas of his colleagues and players. Players were involved in discussing tactics, and club coaches were invited to offer ideas and suggestions during the Stars of the Future courses. Raynor was modest enough to accept the ideas offered, smart enough to know which would work and cunning enough to know when to apply those ideas in practice.

Secondly, he was a master at motivating his players. He became proud of what Sweden achieved and encouraged a sense of nationalism to bolster the team. After Sweden defeated Italy 3–2

in Sao Paulo in the 1950 World Cup, Raynor wrote: 'We knew
we could beat them. For I have never subscribed to the view
that Sweden must always be the underdogs.' Raynor was more
than an honorary Swede: he had become Swedish in his mindset
and used the pride he experienced in being national coach to
foster a strong, team spirit.

Thirdly, he possessed boundless enthusiasm. He took it
on himself to individually coach the great centre half Bertil
Nordahl when he was still playing club football for Degerfors.
Raynor could have simply left this job to the club coach but
instead personally intervened to help develop Nordahl into one
of the best centre halves of his day. One of the great players in
European football history, Kurre Hamrin, remarked that he felt
brainwashed as a result of Raynor's persistence in individually
training Hamrin as a teenager. Raynor would be up at 4 a.m.
and have Hamrin on the training ground at 5 a.m. to go through
drills and crosses and make sure that Hamrin was doing things
'just right'.

Similarly, before the 1950 World Cup, Raynor would
spend hours 'pressure training' Kalle Palmer, a player who was
otherwise overlooked because he was so weak. Sweden enjoyed
the benefits of this intensive training when Palmer got Sweden
to Brazil with his hat-trick against Ireland and then saw the
striker improve still further during the 1950 finals in Brazil.
When Raynor came back to England he twice resurrected the
career of Alick Jeffrey, one of the greatest, if unluckiest, strikers
in England's football history.

Just how Raynor created this climate of success must
be at the heart of any assessment of his life and work. Brian
Glanville calls Raynor 'a guerrilla tactician' using guile and
psychology to overcome the odds but this can in no way be
the conclusive reason for Raynor's success. The first thing one
should note is that whereas George Raynor was proud to be
British, this pride did not blind him to the opportunities that
could be enjoyed when taking on board ideas and initiatives
from wherever they came. What it also shows is that Raynor

accepted that there was a Swedish way of doing things and rather than ignore that and revert to attitudes which had mired the British, he accepted and promoted the Swedish way not only while in Sweden but also when he returned to England. In Sweden these attitudes clearly contributed to success, yet in England the ideas he brought back with him were ignored and rejected.

In Sweden, it was not the done thing to bawl and scream at players. It certainly was not Raynor's way of doing things and he felt his successes more than vindicated the benefit of a pastoral care of his charges. He believed in gentle encouragement rather than castigation and chastisement. Young players were guided to think about how they were playing the game. Raynor would encourage teamwork in simple but effective ways: telling players, for instance, that they should know who they would be passing the ball to before the ball reached them. He also encouraged debate and discussion from players, inviting opinion and ideas so that the players could see that they had responsibilities in the game.

Before the 1958 World Cup Raynor went so far as to stay with each of his squad players, taking time to get to know them and for them to get to know him, to personalise himself in their eyes and develop trust and a bond with the players. While this is not a blueprint for success, and there is no suggestion implied here that such a course of action would result in modern teams being more successful, it does offer an insight into the type of manager and person that George Raynor was.

Raynor also saw the virtue in concentrating on youth development with each of his teams. Circumstances in Sweden, where senior internationals were leaving the country created increased opportunities for young players. This led to Raynor embracing the ideas promoted by the Swedish FA to bring through young stars. Club sides had highly competitive youth programmes, while the Stars of the Future courses and the press matches were programmes that led to Skoglund, Palmer and Hamrin coming to national attention.

In England such programmes did not exist. Indeed, youth football in England was not organised on the same lines as it was in Sweden. In the early 1950s Matt Busby started creating a team known as the Busby Babes. That 'concept', of building a side based on young players, was something of a sensation simply because it challenged what appeared to be the conventional practice where English League clubs relied wholly on seasoned professionals.

The Football Association had schoolboy internationals dating back years but it was only in 1948 that the first FA Youth Cup was instituted, and only in 1954 that a 'young England' team was first gathered to play against international opponents: a direct result of losing to Hungary in previous year.

When Raynor returned to England in 1959 and started coaching Skegness Town he encouraged this sense of opportunity for young players, going to the extent of offering coaching to all clubs in the Skegness area to help their young players start right and keep them on the right track.

This attitude was thoroughly out of keeping with the attitudes in the area and his offer was regarded with suspicion and not welcomed.

Another thing one notices about Raynor was his amiable manner. Although trained as a physical instructor in the British Army, Raynor did not allow himself to become the type of despot that one would associate with graduates of the armed services. Others like Stan Cullis and Sir Matt Busby had worked as Army Physical Training instructors during the war and, for all the regard that both are still held, one gets the distinct impression that neither broached reproach from players. This is very much in keeping with the British view as to what a football manager should be. While at Coventry City, Raynor's style of management was clearly at odds with the accepted culture that managers were no nonsense types who did not welcome back-chat and ruled with an iron fist. Neither the directors of Coventry City, nor the players, had much time for a person who so clearly bucked the trend. Raynor saw Coventry City as a long-term project during which he would be seeking to develop a comprehensive youth programme and build a talented squad that could not only achieve promotion but build on that success. Coventry City saw him as a pushover who wasn't up to the job.

In the final days of his stint as manager of Doncaster Rovers, one reporter remarked at how frustrating it was to have a manager who was so well-liked when some of the players were clearly in need of having football boots kicked at them or having the 'hairdryer' treatment. This said a great deal about the reporter, about British football and also the way Raynor worked.

In *European Football History* Gordon Jeffrey wrote about the melting pot of brains that Raynor gathered during the Stars of the Future courses. It was because of these courses that, in addition to bringing on young players, there was also constant development and thought in the way the Swedes approached the game. This is true. The game in Sweden did develop under Raynor.

During the 1950 World Cup, Raynor believed in an attack-first principle: Sweden, he felt, should take the game to the opponents. He did not believe, at that time, in containment or slowing the game down or playing down the clock as we may well see nowadays. As a result he attacked the Brazil side in the final group and led Sweden to a 7–1 defeat. He insisted on attacking Uruguay when Sweden led 2–1 with 15 minutes to go. This was clearly a principle in need of revision. By the 1958 World Cup, Raynor was exhibiting a much more responsive approach.

In the quarter-final he instructed Nils Liedholm to neutralise the attacking threat of Voinov. In the first-round match against Mexico he played Mellberg as a tough attacking midfielder purposefully to unsettle the Mexico players. There was a constant development to learn and improve the game in Sweden and Raynor was very much at the forefront of that development and programme.

Was George Raynor the best coach England never had? Arguably, yes. However, history records that England ultimately rejected him, ignored his ideas and suffered without him.

In Britain, he is still a little-known figure. He was, nevertheless, a man of great talent and that talent, rightly, should be marked and recorded. I hope that this book has offered some insight into his rightful place in the history of our game.

BIBLIOGRAPHY

Boys Book of Soccer (Evans Publishing, various years)
Buchan, Charles, *A Lifetime in Football* (Sportsmans Book Club, 1955)
Bury Times, 1934–35
Busby, Sir Matt, *Soccer at the Top* (Sphere, 1974)
Coventry Evening Telegraph, 1955
Creek, F.N.S., *Association Football* (Dent, 1937)
Daily Mirror, 1969
Doncaster Evening Post
Evening Standard, 2002
FA Book for Boys (Evans Publishing, various years)
FA Yearbook (Naldrett Publishing, various years)
Ferrier, Bob, *Soccer Partnership* (Sportsmans Book Club, 1961)
Finney, Tom, *My Autobiography* (Headline, 2004)
Glanville, Brian, *Football Memories* (Virgin Books, 1999)
Glanville, Brian, *Soccer Nemesis* (Soccer Book Club, 1955)
Glanville, Brian, *The Story of the World Cup* (Faber & Faber, 2010)
Glanville, Brian & Weinstein, *Jerry World Cup* (Sportsmans Book Club, 1960)
International Football Book (Souvenir Press, various years)
James, Brian, *England v Scotland* (Sportsmans Book Club, 2nd edn, 1970)
Joy, Bernard, *Soccer Tactics* (Soccer Book Club, 1959)
Kock, Putte, *Fotbollen – Mitt Ode* (Gebers, 1955)
Meisl, Willy, *Soccer Revolution* (Soccer Book Club, 1956)
Mortensen, Stanley, *Football is My Game* (Sampson, Low, Marston and Co., 1949)
Raynor, George, *Football Ambassador at Large* (Stanley Paul, 1st edn, 1960)
Raynor, George, *Football Ambassador at Large* (Soccer Book Club, 1960)
Rollin, Jack, *Soccer at War* (Headline Book Publishing, 2nd edn, 2005)
Rous, Stanley, *Football Worlds* (Faber & Faber, 1978)
Skegness Standard, 1960–65

The Big Book of Football Champions (LTA Robinson, various years)
The Times (various years)
Various, *Association Football* (Caxton, 1960)
Various eds, *Book of Football* (Marshall Cavendish partwork, 1971)
Williams, Charlie, *Ee I've had some laughs* (Wolfe Publishing Limited, 1973)
Wilson, Jonathan, *Inverting the Pyramid* (Orion, 2009)
Winterbottom, Walter, *Soccer Coaching* (Heinemann Publishing, 1964)
Wolstenholme, Kenneth, *Young England* (Soccer Book Club, 1959)
Wright, Billy, *Captain of England* (Stanley Paul, 1950)

If you enjoyed this book, you may also be interested in …

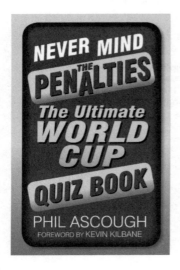

Never Mind the Penalties
PHIL ASCOUGH

England haven't won it since 1966 but every time the World Cup is played, there's always hope that this year will be the year. The World Cup has its critics but time stands still when your team plays. Hope and horror, passion and pain – and that's just the draw for the final groups! *Never Mind the Penalties* is the ultimate collection of World Cup teasers, pulling together the highs and lows, the match-winners and the madness. Author and journalist Phil Ascough has trawled through his own memories, picked the brains of fellow followers and produced a compilation designed to furrow a few eyebrows and also raise a smile. Get your FIFA thinking caps on – it's quiz time!

978 0 7509 5842 4

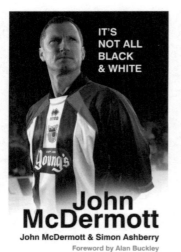

John McDermott
JOHN MCDERMOTT & SIMON ASHBERRY

When John McDermott received the annual PFA Merit Award, in recognition of his record-breaking career at Grimsby Town, he joined an elite group of footballers made up of the likes of Sir Bobby Charlton, Pelé and George Best. He played an incredible 754 games overall for the Mariners and is one of only seventeen players in the history of English football to play more than 600 Football League matches for the same. Now McDermott is lifting the lid for the first time on the career that made him one of the most respected defenders in the Football League.

978 0 7524 9264 3

Visit our website and discover thousands of other History Press books.

www.thehistorypress.co.uk